PACIFIC FORUM

The Pacific Forum was founded in 1975 to promote an international dialogue among thoughtful leaders in the fields of business, government and scholarship. Its principal purpose is to provide a private sector input into the formulation of sound public policies on such vital issues in the Pacific area as economic and social development based on mutual security, political stability, investment, trade and the intelligent use of resources.

The Pacific Forum's seminars, policy studies and publications are of particular value at a time when economic development and social change are moving more rapidly in the Pacific region than in any other area of the world. An informed public understanding of the issues affecting the maintenance of peace and progress is essential to the interests of all countries which daily grow more interdependent in the Pacific Basin.

The Pacific Forum is composed of prominent leaders and experts in business, finance and education, together with former senior government officials. They provide broad guidance for the work program of the Pacific Forum. Several members normally participate in each seminar, thereby providing continuity as well as a wide range of experience in private and public affairs in critiquing the policies, trends and issues under examination.

A number of research and academic institutions experienced in the advanced study of international economic, political and security affairs are institutional members of the Pacific Forum. These institutional connections and the associated Research Council provide a valuable resource base which is drawn upon for the Forum's studies and seminars.

The Pacific Forum is a private tax-exempt organization which relies on public support for continuance of its important work.

Pacific Forum
Suite 1376
190 South King Street
Honolulu, Hawaii 96813

*Financial Deepening
in ASEAN Countries*

Financial Deepening
in ASEAN Countries

George J. Viksnins

PACIFIC FORUM

Distributed by
The University Press of Hawaii:
Order Department
The University Press of Hawaii
2840 Kolowalu Street
Honolulu, Hawaii 96822

Contents

Preface

This work examines the relationship between financial institutions and economic development in Southeast Asia. After the Communist takeover in Indochina, the ASEAN organization (Association of Southeast Asian Nations) has assumed increasing political importance. Its five member countries (Indonesia, Malaysia, the Philippines, Singapore, and Thailand) are strategically located astride air and sea lanes linking the Far East to the Middle East and Europe, and their governments have emphasized repeatedly that they wish to make the region into a zone of peace, freedom, and neutrality. As it enters into its second decade, the ASEAN organization has become more active in the economic sphere as well: regional trade preference schemes are being negotiated and discussions are under way to make the economies of the ASEAN less competitive and more complementary. While trade among the ASEAN countries presently accounts for only about 15 percent of their total trade, a viable network of financial and commercial contacts is being developed.

The term "financial deepening," as used by Professor Edward S. Shaw in his well-known *Financial Deepening in Economic Development* (Oxford University Press, 1973), refers to increased utilization of money and other financial instruments in the modernization process. It can be contrasted to "shallow finance," where financial repression—runaway inflation, government ceilings on interest rates, and extensive regulations on financial institutions—makes money and other financial assets "perilous to hold." Such repressive measures force spending units to hoard stocks of commodities and to resort to barter which has obvious negative consequences for economic growth and development. This study finds that considerable financial deepening has in fact taken place in the ASEAN region during the past several decades. The Indonesian hyperinflation in the 1960's, culminating in Sukarno's overthrow, is a good case study within the region. To put it very simply, the populace was trying to get rid of money about as quickly as the government was printing it.

The other four ASEAN countries have been spared from the ravages of hyper-inflation and considerable financial deepening has taken place. Even in Indonesia, to a certain extent, the financial markets have recovered and money holdings have increased. By and large, the ASEAN group has followed a capitalistic approach to growth and development; while the free market and private enterprise are not exactly flourishing in all of these countries, they do exist. Unlike those of many other "third world" countries, foreign banks have not been nationalized and foreign investment continues to be welcomed, though on increasingly circumscribed terms. In Singapore and Malaysia, foreign banks continue to perform a quantitatively significant commercial banking function, though their share of total banking system assets is declining—quite sharply in the case of Malaysia. The Asian dollar market in Singapore has begun to provide a significant allocative function for the region as a whole.

It can generally be argued that further liberalization and greater competition in the financial markets would yield positive economic benefits to most ASEAN countries. Private domestic saving provides the bulk of investment funds in comparison to government saving or foreign investment. However, the crucial question is whether the ASEAN governments will have the political will to maintain an atmosphere conducive to private saving and investment.

My involvement and scholarly interest in Asian economic development began more than a dozen years ago, when I participated in a project on private foreign investment carried out by the Stanford Research Institute and worked in Thailand for two years for the U.S. economic assistance mission (1968–1970). As a U.S. AID economist, I worked closely with the National Economic Development Board and the Bank of Thailand. In subsequent trips to the ASEAN region in 1976 and 1979, I have benefitted from meetings and discussions with professional colleagues in all five countries. Specifically, I wish to thank the SGV company of multinational accountants for making available data on ASEAN commercial banks, as well as the staffs of Bancom Development Corporation of the Philippines and the Bank of Thailand for bibliographical assistance.

My sponsors and friends at the Pacific Forum provided outstanding support and editorial guidance from the outset of this study; but I assume sole responsibility for errors of fact and interpretation.

George J. Viksnins

Financial Deepening
in ASEAN Countries

CHAPTER 1

Development and
Financial Institutions

The role of financial institutions in the development process has been investigated quite extensively, both from a theoretical and an empirical–historical point of view. The importance of money and finance in a modern exchange economy cannot be exaggerated; indeed, the extent of monetization in a country appears to be one of the best indications of its growth and development. Goldsmith's pioneering work on financial development observes that the "monetization ratio" in practice ranges from 0.2–0.3 in the "Bantu areas of South Africa" to 0.88 in Japan and 0.93 in the U.S.[1] From a purely theoretical point of view, the use of money lowers the cost of each transaction by eliminating the high search and information costs associated with barter. In a non-monetized economy there must be a "double coincidence of wants": a person wishing to sell a chicken and buy rice must find a mirror image—someone wishing to sell rice and buy a chicken. A second problem arises in arranging intertemporal transactions: if you borrow a chicken from the neighbor for a month, what should be the repayment (a fatter chicken, a herd of chickens, or several omelettes)? In the absence of a standardized unit of account, it is also very difficult to compare alternative courses of action: should one follow strategy A, yield three chickens, or strategy B, produce two pigs? Finally, the use of money enables a surplus-producing spending unit to "store value" efficiently. It is undoubtedly this value-storing function that led to the development of money commodities in pre-historic times—metallic coins and the like became a fairly efficient way to store purchasing power or invest surplus income. Basically, the use of money lowers the cost of each transaction, thus increasing a country's output and income. In most of the ASEAN countries covered in this study, the use of money is presently quite well developed; but these countries cannot be considered fully monetized by any means.

To outline further a general theoretical framework, money—defined as any generally accepted medium of exchange—is the most basic financial asset. In any given time period, say, one year, an economic system consists of surplus spending units, those with income greater than expenditure, and of deficit spending units, those wishing to spend in excess of that year's earnings. In an economy where money is the only financial asset, the development of financing is subject to essentially the same problem as with barter of commodities—the need for double coincidence of wants. In a primitive financial market, the deficit spending unit wishing to issue a "primary security," such as a mortgage or an I.O.U., must find a particular surplus spending unit who has an appropriate amount of surplus and who is also willing to acquire primary security. As Gurley and Shaw have put it:

> The rudimentary economy's capacity for growth is limited by its financial system. With no financial asset other than money, there are restraints on saving, on capital accumulation, and on efficient allocation of saving to investment that depress the rate of growth in output and income. Some of the constraints on real growth that are evident in this model are reminiscent of the financial handicaps faced by the American economy about the time of the Revolution and by some underdeveloped countries today.[2]

As the economy grows and develops a surplus of output above subsistence needs, specialized institutions are created to mobilize and allocate such funds. These "financial intermediaries" provide an indirect finance function, issuing secondary securities (bank deposits, insurance policies, and the like), which are acquired by the surplus spending units. In turn, the financial intermediaries allocate these funds to deficit spending units by acquiring their primary securities (stocks and bonds, mortgages, and so on). This process of intermediation has been succinctly summarized by Hugh Patrick:

Financial intermediaries have an important function in providing a market mechanism for the transference of claims on real resources from savers to the most efficient investors. The more perfect are financial markets, the more nearly optimum allocation of investment is achieved. In this way, the financial system accommodates economic growth; on the other hand, to the extent that the financial system is underdeveloped and/or inefficient, it restricts growth below what optimally could be achieved. The mechanism whereby financial institutions effect this transfer is to issue their liabilities (sell indirect securities) to savers, in exchange ultimately for their real saving (assets) or monetary claims upon such assets, and to provide the assets so accumulated to investors by purchasing their primary securities. The financial system can create a wide variety of financial claims (indirect securities) to serve as assets for savers, with claims differentiated by liquidity, yield, maturity, divisibility, risk of default or change in values, and other services. In this way the financial system obtains claims to resources which it provides, under optimal market conditions, to the most efficient user.[3]

Historical experience shows that most countries accumulate financial assets more rapidly than real wealth; according to Gurley and Shaw, the ratio of financial to real wealth ranges from 10–15 percent in countries such as Afghanistan and Ethiopia to 30–60 percent in more prosperous countries, Brazil, Mexico, Korea, Venezuela, to more than 100 percent in Japan, Switzerland, and the U.S.[4] In the same vein, Goldsmith finds that his "financial interrelation ratio" rises more than proportionately with growth in GNP.[5] Monetization and the growth of financial intermediaries are very closely correlated with economic growth and development in market-oriented economies, although the direction of causation is still a matter of some dispute. Considerable discussion has taken place in the literature about whether the growth of financial institutions is "supply leading" or "demand following." While this is akin to the old "chicken–egg" issue, it is to be hoped that works of the present sort will contribute some useful information on this issue.

As one might expect, commercial banks are the most common institutions to develop early in the process of economic growth and industrialization. Banks provide a basic intermediary function between savers and investors, or surplus and deficit spending units. As Cameron has pointed out, commercial banks are unique in being able to supply liquidity to the economy by creating money (at first bank-notes and later checking accounts or demand deposits): "They are in a position not merely to serve as the custodians of the stock of money, but also to increase or decrease that stock. The consequences of this power for society at large can be considerable—and either favorable or unfavorable."[6] In addition, Cameron notes that bankers are also often in a position to assist entrepreneurs or to perform entrepreneurial functions themselves. Germany and Japan, in particular, are often cited as historical examples of close cooperation between aggressive bankers and emerging industrial firms,[7] although some, more recent research has suggested that this comparison may be simplistic.[8]

The theoretical benefits associated with monetization and the growth of financial intermediaries are seldom fully realized in practice, especially in the so-called developing countries or less developed countries (LDCs). In many LDCs, markets for financial assets simply do not exist and often the use of money is less than universally accepted. Even in most of the larger ASEAN countries—say, the Philippines, Thailand, or Indonesia—the bulk of the population will be found in rural areas and engaged primarily in subsistence farming. For the average peasant in such countries, income and consumption are usually quite closely matched. If a particularly good harvest does come along, and/or the "farm-gate" price of the product rises substantially, it is rather unlikely that the resulting surplus income will be saved or transformed into productive investment in most cases. In rural areas of Asia, as well as in most economies of the less developed world, a small surplus of saving may often be used to buy additional consumer goods (to engage in a shopping spree) or for the enhancement of ceremonial–religious activities (a larger dowry, a fancier funeral, or more gold leaf pasted on the village idol). Another very likely use for the surplus lies in the hoarding of precious metals or jewelry. If the surplus is very large, the farmer may consider buying more land, farm animals, or agricultural implements—but, if the supply is relatively fixed, prices of land and investment goods are simply bid up and real investment remains about the same. The idea of traveling to the provincial capital and depositing the funds in a financial institution, probably filling out forms and dealing with often supercilious white-collar clerks perhaps from a different social or tribal group, will not even be considered. These limitations in ASEAN countries contrast with the range of alternatives available to a surplus spending unit in a typical Western city: commercial banks, mutual savings banks, and savings and loan associations on every corner are advertising the attractions of their checking and savings accounts daily; insurance policies and pension plans are being marketed aggressively; mutual funds and brokers of various sorts are calling on the telephone; and so on. In most cases, these specialized financial institutions will mobilize even very small surpluses and, at least in theory, make these funds available to the most credit-worthy borrowers for their most productive investment projects.

In addition to the unavailability and/or inaccessibility of financial institutions, markets in less developed countries often do not allocate funds to the most credit-worthy borrowers for their most efficient projects due to what has been termed "financial repression." This phenomenon has been discussed at length elsewhere,[9] but perhaps the simplest definition of financial repression would be a situation where the average saver is consistently offered a negative real rate of return on financial assets. In other words, in such markets the expected inflation rate is on average above the interest rate paid on deposits and securities, with the latter rate being held below its market-clearing level by government fiat (e.g., usury ceilings, tax provisions, and the like). If the real rate of interest offered by financial institutions becomes negative, the demand for loanable funds shifts to the right and the supply schedule to the left—more simply, everyone wants to borrow and virtually nobody wishes to lend.

Under these conditions, the country's money and capital markets soon become *fragmented* in a number of ways. The first example of this fragmentation is a division between the market for physical capital or durable goods and the market for financial assets. Capital goods in a less developed country often are (or become) as McKinnon has put it, "lumpy, illiquid, and specific to a task."[10] In an industrial country a 1 percent or 2 percent addition to the electric power generating capacity is relatively easy, and there is considerable flexibility in responding to variations in demand. In the provincial capital of a poor country, with a single power plant, the choice may be to increase capacity by 100 percent (by building one more plant of the same size) or to do nothing at all. The owner of a rice mill in rural Sumatra may not be able to "liquidate" his real investment, either partly or as a whole. In other words, he may not be able to borrow against his equity and the market for used machinery may be very imperfect. Surplus spending units simply refuse to hold financial assets, even though the costs of hoarding inventories of commodities or having excess capacity may be, from society's point of view, very high. As U Tun Wai has put it:

> If a developing country does not have adequate financial intermedia-
> tion, then farmers and others living in rural areas do not have much
> opportunity to choose between different forms of savings. They could
> either save in the form of currency or hoard gold or other consumer
> goods, either as a means of protection against inflation or to be certain
> of obtaining the consumer goods when needed. The stocking of com-
> modities by a large section of the consuming public can be very waste-
> ful, however, as, for example, in India, where harvested crops are eaten
> by rodents.[11]

A second example of market fragmentation is the familiar distinction made between the organized and the unorganized money market.[12] As noted above, real interest rates in the organized market are
often negative, producing a chronic situation of excess demand for
loanable funds. In the financially repressed economy the organized
market typically consists of a handful of commercial banks, who have
been granted quasi-monopoly status by the government, and probably also a small group of government credit institutions, whose funds
come from the government (or foreign aid donors) directly. As
McKinnon has put it, "even ordinary government deficits on current
account frequently preempt the limited lending resources of the deposit banks. Financing of the rest of the economy must be met from
the meager resources of money lenders, pawn-brokers, and cooperatives."[13] Financial repression reduces the mobilization of savings,
and also affects the allocation process; low or even negative interest
rates on bank assets will intensify the bank manager's risk aversion
and liquidity preference. It is not really necessary for the banker to
scrutinize the credit-worthiness of the borrower or the benefit–cost
ratio of the proposed project, for a 20 percent inflation rate and a 10
percent usury ceiling will make every borrower a financial genius and
almost every project a profitable one. Thus, bankers are likely to rely
more on non-economic (or quasi-economic) considerations in allocating loanable funds in the organized market. Small amounts of short-
term credit will be granted to safe, established customers (e.g., the
export–import sector), whose collateral is riskless (e.g., bills of
lading, import licenses), after the priority needs of government
finance have been satisfied. Credit allocation on the basis of nepo-
tism, rebates and "kick-backs," political and establishment connec-

tions will tend to supersede economic calculations of project efficiency. Finally, even if we postulate a credit allocation system completely free from all of these abuses—a system with supremely honest bureaucrats just carrying out their mandate, what would probably emerge is a form of "queuing," or a lining-up of credit applications on a first-come, first-served basis, without regard to the merit of the project at the time that the loan is actually made.[14]

A third example of financial market fragmentation is primarily a special case of the distinction made above—namely the urban–rural split. Until very recently, in most ASEAN countries the term "organized money market" in practice meant the "urban money market" or, even more narrowly, the market for loanable funds organized by commercial banks in the capital city. Newlyn points out that "almost without exception the third world countries, whether or not under colonial political domination, have historically been dependent upon financial institutions imposed upon them by the developed countries."[15] As such, early commercial banking development was closely connected with export and import trade, and the national surplus (if any) was often invested in the money markets of the developed countries. The number of commercial banks and bank branches was generally quite limited, and especially so in rural areas. As a result, agricultural finance had to be conducted almost entirely in the so-called unorganized money market. Charles Nisbet found that only about 30 percent of the population had any dealings with financial institutions, and the remainder had access only to money lenders or shopkeepers. This fragmentation produced very high rates of interest in the unorganized rural sector: "most commercial lenders emerge with positive rates ranging from 27 percent to 360 percent, with an annual mean rate of 82 percent."[16] While about half of this lending was for consumption purposes, growth in rural credit to finance expanded production has lagged behind other forms of lending as well.

In the ASEAN countries surveyed in this study, there has been quite a rapid expansion in bank branches located in rural areas—in provincial capitals at least—but these often serve to channel funds back to the capital city. In Thailand, for example, Rozental notes that commercial banks "operate branches in every province of the Kingdom except the Hac Hong Sorn, a remote northwestern area bordering on Burma. Apart from the Bangkok–Thonburi area, there is little correlation between number of persons inhabiting a province and the number of branches. . . ."[17] Despite the fact that interest rates in the unorganized money market average 3 to 5 percent per month in real terms, bank branches in rural areas have often ignored local credit demands. Instead, rural savings are shipped back to the capital city to be used for land speculation, financing of foreign trade activities, and short-term loans to established industrial firms. Thus, "urban bias"[18] operates to fragment the financial markets into a rural and an urban sector, with the former characterized by a large excess demand for credit and high real interest rates, and the latter often developing negative real rates of return and an excess supply of credit for certain favored lines of economic activity (perhaps high technology industries).

Even today, the loan–deposit ratios of most bank branches in the rural areas of the ASEAN countries are below one, and a number of central banks have been forced to make special provisions for agricultural credit. In the words of one Thai commercial banker:

> In the past, commercial banks were not interested in providing loans directly to farmers. However, in 1975 the government set a target that commercial banks must provide agricultural credit to the extent of at least seven per cent of their total deposits at the end of the previous year and now the percentage has been raised to 11 per cent, plus another two per cent for agri-business. At the beginning, the measure was not very effective as small banks could not meet the target. But the situation has improved and the target is likely to be met.[19]

Other types of fragmentation can also be mentioned briefly. In many financially repressed economies there is a sharp separation between assets denominated in the local currency and those denominated in foreign exchange. Individuals and firms holding local currency assets are unable to convert them into other currencies due to exchange controls and other restrictions. On the other hand, those active in the export sector will seldom consider volunteering to convert their foreign exchange back to local money, either because negative real interest rates are offered on assets in the organized money market locally or because these agents anticipate further convertibility controls. Thus, the two markets become fragmented and the flexibility of substitution between the local currency assets and those denominated in foreign exchange is reduced. While the lagging economy may try to overcome such fragmentation by periodic devaluation of the local currency, this often leads to a vicious circle in expectations. As Shaw has expressed it:

Financial repression imposes a consistent bias, then, for export of domestic savings. Its effect, too, is to induce cycles of savings flows, tides in and out that cannot be absorbed by efficient adjustments on current accounts for trade. As excess demand accumulates on the foreign exchanges before a reluctant adjustment of the exchange rate, savers foresee and respond to prospective devaluation. When the devaluation has been done, providing usually a safety margin of undervaluation, savings return. Each return inflates bank reserves, and nominal money increases at a rate that cannot be matched by growth in real money demanded. Then momentum builds toward a new climax of overvaluation and depreciation.[20]

A special case of this phenomenon may be the behavior of certain LDC central banks that tend to hold large foreign exchange reserves, often earning a much lower rate of return on New York or London money market instruments than could be expected on local development projects. In other words, even central bankers may fear that their reserves could lose purchasing power and/or convertibility upon repatriation.

Finally, a financially repressed economy often develops a sharp dichotomy between short-term and long-term financial instruments. In a repressed economy, the planning horizon of savers becomes very short. Since the organized money market is customarily offering very low or even negative rates of return, asset holders will try to maximize their liquidity and avoid being locked in at a negative rate for a long time period. Investors will have to finance capital projects by borrowing large amounts in the short-term money market. Caldwell points out that even in Taiwan, which has a rather well-monetized economy with relatively little financial repression taking place, businessmen often use a postdated check as a device for raising medium-term capital.[21] Rozental found that about one-fourth of business finance in Thailand, another relatively rapidly monetizing economy, had to be raised from family and friends or through informal credit cooperatives in the unorganized money market.[22] This process of financing long-term investments through short-term borrowing is, of course, quite risky and very costly, but the demand for long-term assets often simply does not exist. Government efforts to create long-term instrumentalities, such as setting up a "handsome and expensive stock exchange," seem to be doomed to failure unless monetary reform in the short-term end of the market takes place first. Again to quote Shaw:

The brief for expensive, dramatic action to promote long-term finance is not persuasive. One reason is that opportunity yields for tax revenues or foreign aid to subsidize long-term markets are high. The developing economy does not have much largesse, collected in a more or less neutral fashion, to distribute among numerous claimants including infrastructure and housing or land reform and agriculture as well as finance. Moreover, subsidies have a way of reaching the strongest as distinct from the intended recipients. Finally why lavish resources on long-term finance when deepening at short-term is cheaper?[23]

To conclude, let us spell out some of the practical consequences of financial repression. While the five ASEAN countries are by no means unique in being guilty of extremely repressive measures, they provide an interesting spectrum of experience in this regard, ranging from Singapore, with its sophisticated financial system, to the hinterlands of Indonesia, the Philippines, and Thailand, where even today monetization is proceeding slowly—partly due to past and present financial repression. We have discussed five examples or types of fragmentation in markets: (a) real vs. financial assets markets; (b) the organized market vs. the "curb market" for loanable funds; (c) the urban vs. rural credit market; (d) local currency vs. foreign exchange assets market; and (e) the short-term vs. the long-term market. Usually this multi-faceted fragmentation of the financial markets is due mainly to inflationary monetary and fiscal policies being carried out by the government, coupled with *ad hoc* attempts to escape the consequences of such actions—direct manipulation of credit flows to various sectors and regions, control over interest rates and foreign exchange flows, price ceilings and floors, and so on. To be sure, some other factors do contribute to fragmentation. For example, social and political bottlenecks may prevent the integration of the rural and urban credit markets. Problems of communication and transportation also often exist. However, by and large, government regulations are the chief culprit: real interest rates are kept low by fiat, chartering and branching are restricted, and non-market principles are used in credit allocation.

Financial deepening—more realistic interest rates and greater competition in all markets—would benefit everyone in the long run. Savings mobilization would probably improve (although the interest elasticity of household savings is a debatable issue) as lenders are offered positive interest rates. Average rates charged to borrowers would probably come down as the organized money market is merged with "curb finance," where interest rates of 50 to 100 percent per annum are often charged. As a general rule, the distribution of income would also probably be improved by a better functioning credit market, though the lot of the poorest 20 percent would perhaps change little. Yet, there is little short-run attraction for financial reform. The politically powerful elites generally benefit from existing repressive practices. This situation has been aptly summarized by Edgar Owens and Robert Shaw in their excellent book *Development Reconsidered:*

> Under political pressures from the elite groups that support them, dual society governments have encouraged large-scale, capital-intensive industries and large-farm, mechanized agriculture. Interest rates have been kept low, so that politically favored entrepeneurs are favored with subsidized credit to build cheaply their empires in land or large industries. Foreign exchange has been overvalued so that the rich can import at artificially low prices in terms of their own domestic currencies capital goods such as tractors and steel mills, and luxury items such as air conditioners and automobiles. Wages in the modern large-scale part of the economy have been forced upward, encouraging the use of capital instead of labor. This artificial system of pricing has benefitted the elites at the expense of creating new jobs and accelerating economic growth.[24]

NOTES

1. Raymond W. Goldsmith, *Financial Structure and Development*, pp. 303–307. For more general works on development financing, see Antonin Basch, *Financing Economic Development* as well as A. P. Thirlwall, *Financing Economic Development*. A good series of country studies, though mostly pertaining to the industrialized nations of the so-called First World, is found in Arnold W. Sametz (ed.), *Financial Development and Economic Growth*.

2. John G. Gurley and Edward S. Shaw, *Money in a Theory of Finance*, p. 13. A more formalistic treatment is found in Vicente Galbis, "Financial Intermediation and Economic Growth in Less-Developed Countries," pp. 257–268.

3. Hugh T. Patrick, "Financial Development and Economic Growth in Underdeveloped Countries," p. 182.

4. John G. Gurley and Edward S. Shaw, "Financial Development and Economic Development," pp. 257–268.

5. Goldsmith, *Financial Structure and Development*, Chapter 2.

6. Rondo Cameron (ed.), *Banking and Economic Development*.

7. Hugh T. Patrick, "Japan, 1868–1914." *In* Rondo Cameron, *Banking in the Early Stages of Industrialization,* p. 263.

8. Kozo Yamamura, "Japan 1868–1930." *In* Cameron, *Banking and Economic Development,* pp. 168–198.

9. The two standard works on this are E. S. Shaw, *Financial Deepening in Economic Development* and Ronald I. McKinnon, *Money and Capital in Economic Development.*

10. McKinnon, *Money and Capital,* Chapter 2.

11. U Tun Wai, *Financial Intermediaries and National Savings in Developing Countries,* p. 31. This point is further developed in Patrick, "Financial Development and Economic Growth in Underdeveloped Countries."

12. This distinction was first elaborated in U Tun Wai, "Interest Rates in the Organized Money Markets of Underdeveloped Countries," pp. 249–278.

13. McKinnon, *Money and Capital,* pp. 68–69.

14. For further discussion, see Ali Issa Abdi, *Commercial Banks and Economic Development,* especially pp. 30–31.

15. W. T. Newlyn et al., *The Financing of Economic Development,* p. 326.

16. Charles Nisbet, "Interest Rates and Imperfect Competition in the Informal Credit Market of Rural Chile," p. 76. McKinnon, op. cit., Chapter 7, points out that cheap credit in the organized sector seldom benefits the "little man," who is "confined to getting month-to-month credit from the village storekeepers."

17. Alek A. Rozental, *Finance and Development in Thailand,* p. 166.

18. For further discussion, see also Michael Lipton, *Why Poor People Stay Poor.*

19. Surak Nananukool, "Role of Financial Institutions in Economic Development," p. 422.

20. Edward S. Shaw, *Financial Deepening,* p. 209.

21. J. Alexander Caldwell, "The Financial System in Taiwan," pp. 729–751.

22. Cf. Rozental, *Finance and Development,* Chapter 7. He estimates modal interest rates of 3 to 5 percent per month.

23. Edward S. Shaw, *Financial Deepening,* p. 146.

24. Edgar Owens and Robert Shaw, *Development Reconsidered,* p. 56. Owens and Shaw distinguish between the so-called dual society and the modernizing society, with general popular participation in the development process. They strongly favor agricultural cooperatives as the vehicle for such participation, and cite a number of quite impressive success stories (Japan, Taiwan, Korea) of rural savings-investment mobilization.

CHAPTER 2

Money and Banking
in the ASEAN Countries:
An Overview

It is not generally known that the developing countries taken as a group have experienced very rapid growth during the past quarter-century. As was pointed out in the World Bank's *World Development Report, 1978,* income per capita has been growing by about 3 percent per year in real terms, "with the annual growth rate accelerating from about 2 percent in the 1950's to 3.4 percent in the 1960's." This rate of growth is well above what the so-called advanced countries experienced at a comparable stage a century ago: "income per person grew by less than 2 percent a year in most of the industrialized nations of the West over the 100 years of industrialization beginning in the mid-nineteenth century." Even Japan, widely cited as a miracle of economic growth, only advanced at about 2.5 percent per year over the past century. To be sure, these gains in output per head have not been distributed equally. The "low-income countries" (with GNP per capita below $250) have been growing much more slowly than the "middle-income countries," and large groups of people in the LDCs continue to live in abject poverty.[1] Yet, the overall growth performance of the developing world is impressive; therefore, instead of focusing exclusively on the failures and problems of the past thirty years, development economists should analyze the record of success for lessons to be learned. In this context, the five ASEAN countries provide a useful case in point.

As can be seen in Table 1, all of the ASEAN countries have moved into the middle-income category, by the end of the decade of the 1970s, with growth accelerating in a number of cases. Four out of five (Philippines is the exception) experienced growth rates above the average long-term rate of growth of 3 percent referred to above, and Singapore's 7.5 percent growth rate rivals the success stories of East Asia (Japan, Korea, and Taiwan). The ASEAN group seems to have adjusted remarkably well to the turbulent events of the 1970s; as we can note from Table 1, Singapore and Thailand have seen some diminution in growth, but the others have not.

If we project the growth rates of the past seventeen years until 1990, Singapore's GNP per capita would easily reach present European or American levels, Malaysia would near $1500 per year in real terms, and the other three countries would all climb to the above $500 range.

In attempting to analyze the sources of growth in the ASEAN countries, or even in Asia more generally, certain non-economic factors cannot be ignored. In the case of Japan, Korea, and Taiwan, close cooperation between government and business, a clear-cut sense of national purpose and unity, and perhaps even a certain "siege mentality" seem to be considerably more important than economic variables in explaining their growth performance. In sharp contrast to these countries of East Asia, most of the nations of South Asia seem to be beset by internecine struggles and racial–religious rivalries, which at times break into armed conflict (e.g., Bangladesh) or leave entire regions outside effective central control (e.g., the Shan states in Burma). The ASEAN countries seem to present a middle-ground of sorts in terms of such political and social integration.

TABLE I

GNP Growth in ASEAN

	1978 GNP Per Capita (US$)	1960–1976 Growth Rate* (percent)	1970–1977 Growth Rate* (percent)
Singapore	$3,260	7.5	6.6
Malaysia	1,090	3.9	4.9
Philippines	510	2.4	3.7
Thailand	490	4.6	4.1
Indonesia	360	3.1	5.7

*In real per capita terms
SOURCE: *The World Bank Atlas, 1979,* (Washington, D.C.: IBRD).

In purely economic terms, one can consider some of the standard macroeconomic indicators given in Table 2 as explanatory variables. Clearly, the ASEAN countries are all approaching very high levels of savings and investment, in contrast to markedly lower rates found in the less successful countries of South Asia. While a high level of investment in itself does not guarantee economic growth, for projects may turn out to be unproductive and simply add to excess capacity, a nation's willingness to abstain from present consumption and to plan for the future is a prerequisite for entrepreneurial activity and technological progress. Government spending, as a percentage of GNP, varies considerably among the ASEAN countries as well as in South Asia. In the former group, both Malaysia and Singapore rely much more on public sector production than do Indonesia or Thailand, despite the fact that government interference with the free market is minimal in Singapore and nearly maximal in Indonesia. Similarly, Sri Lanka, until recently at least, was almost a textbook example of counter-productive governmental controls, but the level of government spending in Sri Lanka is less than half of what it is in Burma (which remains another such example). Afghanistan, too, had a lower level of government spending in 1975 than any of the countries listed in Table 2, though that will undoubtedly change rapidly under direct Soviet tutelage. Finally, the ASEAN countries have all been quite open to foreign trade and investment, though nationalis-

TABLE 2

Macroeconomic Ratios for Selected Asian Countries, 1975
(expressed as percent of GNP)

ASEAN	Savings	Investment	Government Expenditures	Exports
Indonesia	20.9	19.8	11.8	23.0
Malaysia	22.2	21.1	31.4	60.0
Philippines	25.1	24.8	19.4	17.0
Singapore	27.1	32.9	23.0	99.0
Thailand	22.6	21.8	15.5	17.0
South Asia				
Afghanistan	n.a.	n.a.	10.2	10.0
Burma	6.6	7.0	59.8	8.0
India	12.5*	19.8	39.1	5.0
Pakistan	n.a.	15.7	33.7	9.0
Sri Lanka	10.0	15.4	28.6	18.0

*Net national savings
SOURCE: Asian Development Bank, *Key Indicators of Developing Member Countries of ADB,* October 1976.

tic considerations have played a strong role in policy-making in these areas. The costs and benefits of export-oriented growth versus an import substitution strategy have been discussed at length elsewhere,[2] but there can be little doubt that the outward-looking countries of the ASEAN have grown more rapidly than the more inward-looking countries of South Asia. Whether such economic growth has also maximized universal happiness is an issue beyond the scope of this study.

To summarize briefly, the ASEAN countries have, by and large, followed the "capitalist-roader" model of growth and development. Of course, the strict laissez-faire attitudes of nineteenth-century textbooks are nowhere to be found, and the politicians stress national interest and social justice much more than economic efficiency. Yet, the ASEAN countries have relied on market forces for allocation and an economy integrated into the world trading system. This model also emphasizes savings and capital formation, decisions concerning both being left largely to the private sector.[3] Reliance on household saving formation, of course, as argued in the preceding section, involves the functioning of financial institutions and the money market, which brings us to the main subject of this study: financial deepening in the ASEAN countries. Table 3 summarizes recent developments in the monetization of the five countries.

The period selected for inclusion in Table 3 ranges from 1965 to 1978, a relatively short period of time beset by economic and political dislocations in this part of the world. Various considerations, however, make it difficult to cover a longer period of time: the political separation of Singapore and Malaysia in 1965 and the Indonesian hyper-inflation, which peaked in 1968–1969, make it difficult to develop a consistent set of statistics for a longer time span. (The data for Indonesia appear strange as is.) Moreover, the earlier post–World War II developments have been competently treated elsewhere in the literature.[4]

As a general overview, Table 3 shows a very rapid rise in the use of money in the ASEAN countries during this period. In relative terms, the most rapid rise occurred in Indonesia, where the nominal money supply grew nearly a thousand-fold from 1965 to 1978; even after adjusting for officially measured inflation, "real money" holdings rose 34 times in that country. Currency outstanding as a percentage of the money supply fell from nearly 70 percent to 50 percent, indicating a greater willingness on the part of the public to use the services of the

TABLE 3
Selected Measures of Monetization in the ASEAN Countries, 1965–1978

	Indonesia (billions)		Malaysia (millions)		Philippines (billions)		Singapore (millions)		Thailand (billions)	
	1965	1978	1965	1978	1965	1978	1965	1978	1965	1978
GNP (local currency)*	24	20,942	8,582	34,608	23.4	170.9	n.a.	17,406	84.3	442.0
Real GNP (local currency, 1975 prices)	6,477	15,561	12,143	28,658	65.9	137.5	4,639	16,875	139.9	374.5
Money Supply (M1)	2.6	2,488.3	1,517	7,242	2.596	16,946	882	4,926	12.9	54.0
GNP/Money Supply	9.2	8.4	5.6	4.8	9.0	10.1	n.a.	3.5	6.5	8.2
Quasi-money (M2)	2.7	3,929.1	2,457	17,520	4.803	40.344	1,649	10,862	20.8	179.7
GNP/Quasi-money	8.9	5.3	3.5	2.0	4.9	4.2	n.a.	1.6	4.0	2.4
Real Money (M1/P)	51.0	1,730.4	2,305.5	6,420.2	7,231.2	13,574.9	1,544.6	4,642.8	23.4	44.6
Real Quasi-money (M2/P)	52.9	2,732.3	5,876.2	15,531.9	13,378.8	32,746.8	2,887.9	10,237.5	37.4	148.5
M2/M1 (real terms)	1.04	1.58	2.00	2.42	1.85	2.41	1.87	2.20	1.60	3.33
Currency outside banks	1.8	1,239.9	846	3,578	1.483	8.135	469	2,583	8.1	34.0
C/M1	0.69	0.50	0.56	0.49	0.57	0.48	0.53	0.52	0.63	0.63
Monetization (SDRs per capita)	.108	33.2	87.3	468.9	38.6	90.4	285.1	1,653.9	32.3	150.0

*In Indonesia, the local currency is the *rupiah*, pegged at 415 to the dollar from 1972 to 1977; in 1978, 442 to the U.S. dollar was the average rate, while its devaluation relative to other currencies was more substantial (Rp. 504.1 was the average rate in 1977 but 1 SDR = 814.2 Rp. in 1978). For Malaysia, the *ringgit* was approximately 3.06 to the U.S. dollar (and the SDR) in 1965; in 1978, SDR = 2.874 ringgits and US$1 = 2.316. The Philippines' *peso* was 3.9149 to the dollar in 1965, but in 1978, P7.375 = $1 and P9.6202 = 1 SDR. The *Singapore dollar* was quoted at 3.06 in 1965, but 2.274 to the U.S. dollar in 1978 (1 SDR = 2.816 S$). The *baht* of Thailand has been effectively pegged at just above twenty to the U.S. dollar throughout this period (1978, US$1 = 20.336 and 1 SDR = 26.564).
SOURCE: International Monetary Fund, *International Financial Statistics*, various issues.

banking system. In real terms, greater sophistication in using financial institutions is also indicated by the rise in the M2/M1 ratio. While M1 includes currency and demand deposits, M2 adds time and savings accounts in commercial banks to that total. Since the ratio rises from 1.04 to 1.58 during this period of time, Indonesians are increasing their use of the banking system both in the form of checking and fixed deposits. Yet, if we translate Indonesia's M2 total into SDRs* per capita, total money held per head comes out to be only about SDR33 (a little more than US$40), significantly below money holdings in other ASEAN countries. The same conclusion is gotten by looking at the two "velocity" numbers, GNP/M1 and GNP/M2, which are substantially higher for Indonesia—perhaps indicating rather sharp memories of the hyper-inflation period, when money was perilous to hold.

Malaysia, in rather sharp contrast, has experienced considerably greater monetization during this period. M2 holdings per capita are at about US$500, and the two velocity statistics are low and have fallen substantially during the 1970s. The ratio of GNP to M2 has declined from 3.5 in 1965 to 2.0 in 1978, indicating a rise in liquid asset holdings. Malaysia's ratio of M2/M1 at 2.42 is the highest in the region (except, somewhat inexplicably, that of Thailand at 3.33 which does not begin to reach Malaysia's monetization levels in terms of other indicators). Interestingly, in all of the ASEAN countries, the ratio of currency outside banks to the money supply (M1) has remained quite high: in the 50 percent to 60 percent range, compared to the 20 percent to 25 percent in the case of Japan and the U.S., showing that cash transactions are at least as important as those involving payment by checks.

The financial development of the Philippines seems to be lagging behind that of the other ASEAN countries to some extent (with per capita money holdings at about SDR90). While real GNP has more

---

*SDRs (Special Drawing Rights) are a unit of account for official reserve valuations and transactions created by the International Monetary Fund in January 1971. Sometimes called "paper gold," though rather infrequently so nowadays, an SDR was equal to the par value of the U.S. dollar from 1971 to July 1974. Since then the value of the SDR has been tied to a "basket" of 16 currencies, which are valued at their market exchange rates for the dollar and the U.S. dollar equivalents are summed to yield the U.S. dollar rate for the SDR, e.g., at the end of 1978, 1SDR = US $1.30279. Since July 1978, the basket of currencies has included Iran and Saudi Arabia, replacing Denmark and South Africa.

than doubled during the 1965–1978 period, the ratio of "real" M1 in 1978 is only 1.88 times as great as in 1965. The velocity figure for M1 is also the highest in the region, having risen from the already high value of 9.0 in 1965 to 10.1 in 1978; similarly, the M2-velocity is second only to Indonesia's. This probably indicates a certain reluctance on the part of both Indonesians and Filipinos to hold financial assets denominated in a depreciating currency.

Both the Indonesian rupiah and the Philippines' peso have suffered formal devaluations during this period, and both countries have experienced inflation rates well above those of their neighbors. The rate of price increase in Indonesia is an astounding 2700 percent during this time span, though that includes several years of runaway inflation coupled with remarkable price stability in the early 1970s. In the Philippines, the consumer price index has more than tripled since the mid-1960s. In Thailand, approximately in line with the rest of the world, prices in 1978 are 118 percent higher than they were in 1965, and the baht's purchasing power has remained relatively stable. In Malaysia and Singapore, prices are 71 percent and 86 percent higher in 1978, which is better than the world average inflation rate and which is also reflected in the superior performance of the Malaysian ringgit and the Singapore dollar in world money markets. Malaysia accepted the convertible currency provisions of Article VIII of the International Monetary Fund's Articles of Agreement in November 1968, and the Singapore dollar is *de facto* convertible because of its Currency Board arrangement (and it is also a signatory to Article VIII). Both of these currencies were 3.06 to the U.S. dollar at the beginning of the period shown in Table 3, but the ringgit appreciated to 2.316 to the dollar and the Singaporean currency stood at 2.274 to the U.S. dollar in 1978.

As noted above, Singapore has become a major international financial center in recent years, a fact also reflected in the domestic financial statistics shown in Table 3. In terms of industrial as well as financial development, Singapore has little in common with its ASEAN colleagues, save geographic location. Its per capita holdings of near-money (M2) stand at SDR1650, more than three times the Malaysian level and more than ten times the monetization level in Thailand, which is in third place on this score. Singapore's M1-velocity is lower than in the U.S. and only slightly higher than in Japan. Yet, the ratio of currency outside the banking system to conventionally defined money stock (M1) remains at more than one-half, showing that the preference for cash transactions remains high, as in many traditional societies. Also, the ratio of M2/M1 is fairly low relative to a number of other ASEAN countries, indicating that commercial bank time and savings deposits are not as popular in Singapore as elsewhere. However, in this case, the relatively low M2/M1 ratio may indicate greater acceptance of other money substitutes and/or even longer term financial assets than elsewhere in the ASEAN region. After all, with a per capita M2 balance of more than US$2,000, the average Singaporean may be more interested in adding stocks, bonds, insurance and pension claims, and the like, to his portfolio.

Turning finally to Thailand, we encounter a middle-of-the-road case. As noted above, both Indonesia and the Philippines have suffered from a depreciating currency, while the Thai baht has remained relatively stable vis-à-vis its major trading partners. While in 1965 Thailand's M2 balance per capita was considerably lower than in the Philippines, in 1978 it is substantially higher. Its performance on the inflation front is also somewhat better, with a much lower compound growth rate in M1 expansion than either Indonesia or the Philippines. Nevertheless, the Thai people seem to favor cash transactions more than others in the ASEAN region, Thailand having the highest ''currency ratio'' of all, at 0.63 in 1965 as well as in 1978. Growth in M1 is much smaller than growth in M2. A possible explanation for this phenomenon is the rapid growth of the finance companies in the early 1970s, who were able to offer the entrenched commercial banks some real competition for fixed-term deposits, forcing interest rates higher than they would have been otherwise. More discussion on this point will be found in a subsequent section.

In the process of monetization and financial deepening, the primary financial institution to develop is the commercial bank, which is able to issue money and quasi-money assets for the emerging surplus spending units. In most of the ASEAN countries, the financial system continues to be dominated by a limited number of commercial banks, although other financial intermediaries are beginning to emerge. As can be seen in Table 4, total commercial bank assets reached $63 billion at the end of 1977, with roughly two-fifths of the total in banks in Singapore. The total number of commercial banks is 249, divided among 167 domestic banks and 82 foreign owned. More than half of all the foreign-owned banks have been chartered in Ma-

TABLE 4
Commercial Banks in the ASEAN Countries, 1977

	Total Assets in billions of U.S. dollars	Number of Banks (Branches)		Total Assets' Shares (percent)	
		Domestic	Foreign	Domestic	Foreign
Indonesia	9.5	90(951)	11(20)	91†	9
Malaysia	9.2	20(313)	17(148)	56	44
Philippines*	9.6	28(1,197)	4(9)	89	11
Singapore*	25.1	13(131)	37(107)	26	74
Thailand	9.6	16(1,180)	13(19)	94	6
TOTAL	$63.0	167	82	n.a.	n.a.

*In addition, there were 27 and 16 off-shore banks, respectively, operating in Singapore and the Philippines at the end of 1977. Total assets, not included above, were $8.2 billion in Singapore and less than $1 billion for the Phillipines.
†Statistic based on coverage of 65 of the 90 domestic banks.
SOURCE: The SGV Group, *A Study of Commercial Banks in the ASEAN Countries,* December 31, 1977.

laysia and Singapore, while more than half of the locally owned banks are found in Indonesia. There are slightly more than 4,000 bank branches operating within the ASEAN region, with domestic bank branches accounting for roughly 90 percent of the total. Foreign banks are of enormous importance to the economy of Singapore, accounting for nearly three-fourths of total banking system assets, partly in connection with Asian Currency Unit (ACU) operations carried out in the Singapore money market. They are also quite significant in Malaysia, where 17 foreign-owned banks own about 44 percent of banking system assets; but their quantitative importance in the remaining three nations of the ASEAN region appears to be minimal. In Thailand, particularly, the share of total banking business carried on by foreign banks, many of which have long operated there, is a mere 6 percent and the number of foreign bank branches (19) is miniscule compared to the branching permitted to locally-owned banks (there were 1,180 at the end of 1977). In the Philippines, where one often hears complaints about American domination of business and finance, a total of 4 foreign banks operate 9 branches (only 2 of the 4 are American, Citibank, and BoA), while 28 domestic banks have 1,197 branch offices. Indonesia portrays much the same picture, with 91 percent of total banking system assets in locally owned banks. It is certainly tempting to conclude that the superior record of Malaysia and Singapore in financial deepening and their ability to reap the benefits of an appreciating currency in world money markets is in large part due to the competitive discipline provided by a significant number of foreign bank branches.

Concluding this section, Tables 5 and 6 provide an overview of the largest domestic banks operating in the ASEAN area and their relative importance in terms of banking system assets, deposits, and net worth. The largest commercial bank in the region is privately owned Bangkok Bank, which accounts for a full one-third of total deposits held by Thailand's commercial banking system. It is second in terms of net worth, but third in the number of branch offices. The second-place position is occupied by the Philippine National Bank, PNB is 99.5 percent government owned; but it places first in terms of net worth, perhaps due to its long history, which goes back to 1916. Its position of pre-eminence in the commercial banking system of the Philippines has been eroded somewhat in recent years,[5] but it is interesting to note that no other Filipino bank appears in Table 5. The next four places on the list are occupied by four large Indonesian,

TABLE 5

Twenty Largest Commercial Banks in the ASEAN Countries, December 1977
(in millions of U.S. dollars)

	Bank (no. of branches)	Total Assets	Deposits	Net Worth
•TP	Bangkok Bank (202)	$3,336.1	2,428.2	186.3
PG	Philippine National Bank (186)	2,610.3	1,099.9	230.8
IG	Bank Bumi Daya (77)	2,186.3	1,300.2	55.2
IG	Bank Rakyat Indonesia (273)	1,665.9	803.7	101.0
IG	Bank Dagang Negara (70)	1,601.0	543.9	72.9
IG	Bank Negara Indonesia 1946 (214)	1,596.3	902.9	120.2
MG	Bank Bumiputra Malaysia Berhad (52)	1,595.4	1,251.5	49.8
MP	Malayan Banking Berhad (110)	1,448.5	1,097.9	85.7
SM	Development Bank of Singapore (12)	1,419.2	502.1	61.9
SP	Overseas-Chinese Banking Corp. (18)	1,318.0	1,052.7	130.5
SP	United Overseas Bank (26)	1,261.5	667.8	138.9
TM	Krung Thai Bank (154)	1,245.4	1,061.1	68.2
TP	Thai Farmers Bank (170)	919.8	779.0	52.7
SP	Overseas Union Bank (26)	901.2	611.3	51.0
IG	Bank Ekspor Impor Indonesia (46)	771.4	475.5	52.8
MP	United Malayan Banking Corp. Berhad (39)	730.4	524.0	30.0
SP	Chung Kiaw Bank (16)	554.4	407.5	28.5
TP	Bank of Ayudhya (108)	532.1	432.5	39.8
TP	Siam Commercial Bank (79)	520.0	407.5	32.7
MP	United Asian Bank Berhad (28)	504.2	284.8	n.a.

•Key: I = Indonesia; M = Malaysia; P = Philippines; S = Singapore; T = Thailand (first column). G = government-owned; P = privately owned; M = mixed (second column). (The Development Bank of Singapore is 49% government-owned and the Krung Thai Bank is 90% owned by the Thai government.)
SOURCE: The SGV Group, *A Study of Commercial Banks in the ASEAN Countries*, December 31, 1977.

TABLE 6
Banking Concentration in the ASEAN, 1977
(in millions of U.S. dollars)

	Indonesia	Malaysia	Philippines	Singapore	Thailand
Total deposits	4,854.6	6,282.3	4,792.0	13,741.9	7,282.0
Largest domestic bank	1,300.2	1,251.5	1,099.9	1,052.7	2,428.2
(as % of total)	(26.8)	(19.9)	(22.9)	(7.7)	(33.3)
Four largest banks	3,550.7	3,158.2	1,909.2	2,833.9	4,700.8
(as % of total)	(73.1)	(50.3)	(39.8)	(20.6)	(64.6)
Ten largest banks	4,208.3	3,563.7	3,052.3	3,710.9	6,446.4
(as % of total)	(86.7)	(56.7)	(63.7)	(27.0)	(88.5)

SOURCE: The SGV Group, *A Study of Commercial Banks in the ASEAN Countries,* December 31, 1977.

state-owned commercial banks with extensive branching networks. All four of these account for 73.1 percent of total deposits in Indonesia, leaving relatively little business for that country's eight private foreign-exchange banks and almost eighty strictly domestic commercial banks to divide among themselves. Next, the government-controlled Bank Bumiputra Malaysia Berhad (BBMB) has pulled ahead of the privately owned Malayan Banking Berhad in total assets. This is in large part due to the Malaysian government's desire to involve in the economic growth process "bumiputras" (literally translated as "sons of the soil"; native Malays as opposed to the business-oriented Chinese or Indians). However, the BBMB management also deserves credit for an active policy of expansion into rural areas: as of the end of 1967, the bank had 9 branches in operation,[6] but today it has 52. It can also be noted that the Malayan Banking Berhad experienced a serious liquidity crisis in 1966, which has probably impeded its growth. As can be seen from Table 6, the concentration ratio is also quite high in Malaysian commercial banking, with the top four banks accounting for slightly more than half of total deposits.

Singapore, again, provides a rather sharp contrast to the rest of the ASEAN region. Forty-nine percent of the largest commercial bank, the Development Bank of Singapore, is government owned. Organized in July 1968, it accounts for only 7.7 percent of total deposits, despite its rather special position. The Overseas-Chinese Banking Corporation and the similarly oriented United Overseas Bank are privately owned and have a very strong net worth position, ranking fourth and third, respectively, in the ASEAN region. The highly competitive nature of commercial banking in Singapore can be noted by looking at the statistics in Table 6; the top four banks cover 20.6 percent of bank deposits, and even the top ten banks account for only a little more than one-fourth of the total. On the other hand, in Thailand, as already noted, the Bangkok Bank has fully one-third of total bank deposits. Together with the government-controlled Krung Thai Bank, it accounts for 48 percent of deposits.[7] Furthermore, the top four banks hold 64.6 percent, and the top ten, a whopping 88.5 percent in deposits—the highest ratio among the ASEAN states. In general, therefore, Thailand rivals Indonesia for having the least scope for competition in the banking field, although in Thailand the top banks are largely private; their pre-dominance *may* be due to economic efficiency and not to governmental power to restrict entry. Of course, since no new local bank has been chartered in Thailand since 1965—Krung Thai was created in 1966 by combining two existing banks—one suspects a combination of both forces may be at work. Discussions of the financial system of each ASEAN country and then a general summary follow this overview.

NOTES

1. The World Bank, *World Development Report, 1978*, p. 3.

2. Especially relevant is the discussion at the 10th Pacific Trade and Development Conference, March 19–23, 1979, to be found in Ross Garnaut (ed.), *ASEAN in a Changing Pacific and World Economy*. Foreign trade issues are also extensively treated in John Wong, *ASEAN Economies in Perspective* (Philadelphia, Pa.: Institute for the Study of Human Issues, 1979). Two previous Pacific Forum volumes are also directly relevant: Lloyd R. Vasey and George J. Viksnins (eds.), *The Economic and Political Growth Pattern of Asia Pacific* and Lloyd R. Vasey (ed.), *ASEAN and a Positive Strategy for Foreign Investment*.

3. In most of Asia, household saving provides from one-half to two-thirds of gross domestic saving (business and government saving, if any, account for the remainder). For further detail see Lee Hock Lock, *Household Saving in West Malaysia and the Problem of Financing Economic Development*. For a discussion of the Japanese experience, see Tuvia Blumenthal, *Saving in Postwar Japan*. Cross-section studies of Asian savings behavior have found a surprisingly high marginal propensity to save, but suggest that corporate and government saving will have to bear ''an even greater burden'' in the future. Cf. Jeffrey G. Williamson, ''Personal Saving in Developing Nations,'' pp. 343–362.

4. See Robert F. Emery, *The Financial Institutions of Southeast Asia* and Sixto K. Roxas, *Managing Asian Financial Development*.

5. In 1968, the PNB accounted for 31 percent of banking system deposits, while currently this stands at 22.9 percent. Cf. Robert F. Emery, *The Financial Institutions of Southeast Asia,* p. 385.

6. Ibid., p. 279.

7. Emery notes that in 1969 these two banks held 41 percent of all bank assets, which suggests that concentration in Thai banking is increasing. Cf. ibid., p. 567. In 1978, one new foreign bank (European Asian) opened for business, and there was some discussion of chartering some additional banks with regional head offices in 1979.

CHAPTER 3
Indonesia

Perhaps the single most controversial issue in any discussion of Indonesia's economic history in its post-independence period is whether, on balance, economic and social conditions have been better under President Sukarno or under pro-Western President Suharto. On September 30, 1965, the PKI (the Indonesian Communist Party) attempted a coup or *putsch* against the armed forces, executing six army generals; those who avoided execution organized a violent counter-coup against the Communists, which eventually resulted in a blood-bath involving political opponents of the military, and, more often than not, against Indonesia's Chinese minority.[1] Many regard the overthrow of Sukarno's pro-Communist, extremely anti-Western, and economically inefficient regime as being of great potential benefit to the Indonesian people. Others do not.[2] It is certainly to be granted that Suharto's "New Order" has not benefitted all segments of Indonesian society equally; but one must admit that Sukarno's "Guided Democracy" tended to produce lots and lots of monuments and marginally productive economic projects and little else than hyper-inflation.

In purely economic terms, real net national product increased at an average annual rate of only 1.7 percent, compared to a population growth rate of about 2.4 percent per year; thus, per capita real income fell during the 1958–1965 period. According to Robert Emery, consumer prices, however, really accelerated during this time span, increasing by nearly 600 percent during calendar 1965, and by 1,523 percent from mid-1965 to mid-1966.[3] The rupiah exchange rate, established at 3.8 to the U.S. dollar at time of independence, fell to 143 to the dollar by 1960, and to 5,747 to the dollar by 1964. A massive devaluation took place in December 1965, when the government introduced the New Rupiah at a 1,000:1 ratio. A period of multiple exchange rates and foreign exchange controls followed in the late 1960s. In the opinion of most observers, it was riddled with abuse and administrative difficulties. On April 17, 1970, the exchange rate structure was simplified and a basic general exchange rate of Rp. 378=US$1 was introduced. The Suharto regime also granted operating licenses to a dozen foreign-owned banks and permitted sharp rises in the rate of interest. The five large state banks which had been briefly amalgamated into a Soviet-type state uni-bank in 1965 were separated again. Loan rates at these banks were in the 3 to 5 percent per month range as of October 1967 (i.e., as high as 60 percent simple annual interest), with deposit interest at only 12 to 30 percent per year. Emery also states that private commercial bank rates ranged from 6 to 15 percent per month on loans, and these also offered 4 to 15 percent per month on time deposits. Loan rates charged by credit cooperatives stood at 15 to 16 percent per month and 17 to 20 percent at the *pasar* (market) banks and private money lenders.[4] Thus, despite an inflation rate of 120 percent in 1968, some borrowers were being charged a positive real interest rate. Obviously, the money market became highly fragmented during this period; borrowers with access to the government-supported banks could re-deposit funds with private commercial banks at a profitable premium.

Nevertheless, the money supply explosion was brought under some control by the "New Order" authorities: the money supply rose by 750 percent in 1966, 147 percent in 1967, 116 percent in 1968, and "only" 59 percent in 1969. Quite remarkably, the inflation rate in that year fell to only 16 percent. This suggests that sharply higher interest rates and the prospect of relative stability—not absolute stability—in the money stock is enough to induce spending units to hold onto their cash balances and to use the services of the banking system. After all, barter transactions and illegal foreign exchange dealings are very costly from an economic point of view. During the 1970s, money growth and inflation have been moderate, by Indonesian standards. The money supply growth rate in 1972 was 48 percent, but in both 1976 and 1977, it was under 30 percent. While single-digit inflation rates were not reached, money demand has greatly increased. In fact, the Central Bank felt that some easing in credit terms was necessary in 1978. In the words of H. W. Arndt:

> With the decline in the rate of inflation over the last two years, constant nominal rates of interest have implied higher real rates. In order to alleviate possible adverse effects on investment, the Central Bank at the end of December announced a reduction in bank lending rates, as part of a package of monetary measures. The range of lending rates was, in effect, compressed (from 9–24 per cent to 9–21 per cent) by reducing the higher rates for lower priority areas while keeping the concessionary rates for high priority activities unchanged.[5]

As can be seen from Table 7, the banking system in Indonesia is dominated by the five state-owned "domestic foreign exchange banks" mentioned in the previous section. These five account for 82.4 percent of banking system assets, and foreign banks (including one joint venture) for 9.4 percent, leaving an 8.2 percent share for privately owned Indonesian banks. The largest of these five banks, the Bank Bumi Daya (loosely translated as Agricultural Development Bank), is the former State General Bank (Bank Umum Negara), which was established in 1959 at the time that the Nationale Handels

TABLE 7
Banks in Indonesia, 1977
(in billions of rupiahs)

		Amount	Percent Share
Domestic foreign-exchange banks			
Bank Bumi Daya		907.3	23.0
Bank Rakyat Indonesia		691.3	17.5
Bank Dagang Negara		664.4	16.9
Bank Negara Indonesia 1946		662.4	16.8
Bank Ekspor Impor Indonesia		320.1	8.1
State-owned		3,245.7	82.4
National private (8 banks)		169.8	4.3
Branches of foreign banks and joint venture (11 banks)		370.7	9.4
Selected domestic banks*		153.1	3.9
	Rp.	3,939.3	100.0%

*Includes 52 of the 77 domestic banks not having foreign exchange powers; the excluded banks were smaller than Rp. 600 million in asset size and did not have suitable financial statements.
SOURCE: The SGV Group, *A Study of Commercial Banks in Indonesia, 1977.*

Bank, a private Dutch bank, was nationalized (early in 1965 the British-owned Chartered Bank was amalgamated). Its specialization in lending covers agricultural estates, forestry activities, and the pharmaceutical industry.[6] Over the years, the Bank Bumi Daya has been extensively subsidized by the central bank; even in 1977, when its total assets stood at more than Rp. 900 billion, its deposits totalled Rp. 539 billion. A rather striking example of one of its borrowers is the case of PTP XXX Subang, a former Dutch plantation of some 23,000 hectares, of which only 7,300 are said to be still productive. Half of this area consists of rubber, but the yield has fallen from 1,250 kg/ha in 1953 to 162 kg/ha in 1978, with tea yields also declining sharply. As reported by Howard Dick:

> By 1978 the plantation had contracted debts of billions of rupiahs, but was able to continue making losses at the rate of Rp 37 million per month by borrowing from government banks, not least Bank Bumi Daya. The moral of the episode is not the obvious one of graft and mismanagement. Rather, it is that the state plantation system permits an enterprise so hopelessly uneconomic as PTP XXX Subang to operate at a heavy loss for so long and yet survive on funds borrowed from state banks.[7]

The management of the BBD was changed somewhat in 1977 ''amidst rumors that one-third of the bank's debts were likely to prove irrecoverable.''[8] The Bank Rakyat Indonesia (Indonesian People's Bank) has a rather long history, going back to an 1896 bank that had been organized to provide credit to government officials. In 1958 a Farmers' and Fishermen's Bank was organized, and was merged with the BRI in 1960, when the Netherlands Trading Society and its 17 branches were also added. At the present time, it extends credit mainly in the agricultural area as indicated by its extensive branch network. In the mid-1960s it set up some 500 sub-branches at the sub-district *(katjamatan)* level, but this operation proved very costly and was abandoned. The Bank Dagang Negara (BDN) goes back to the Dutch Excompto Bank, which was established in 1857. It is currently engaged mainly in financing of export production, mining, and miscellaneous other credits. The BDN, along with the Bank of Indonesia (the central bank) itself, was heavily involved in financing Pertamina projects. For sources of funds, it is heavily reliant upon bank borrowings; total assets at the close of 1977 stood at Rp. 664 billion, but deposits were Rp. 226 billion. The Bank Negara Indonesia (State Bank of Indonesia) was established in July 1946, and appears to have been intended as the new republic's central bank and bank of issue. However, after independence, it was decided that the Bank of Java (established in 1827 by the Dutch) would continue to serve its central role as the bank of issue. The government bought the Bank of Java from its shareholders, and the BNI developed as a commercial bank, though a great many government enterprises have accounts with it. Finally, the Bank Exspor Impor Indonesia was part of Unit II of the Soviet-style, state bank organized in 1965 (along with BRI). At the end of 1968, the two were separated. As the name implies, the BEII is involved in foreign trade financing, but also accepts deposits (unlike the U.S. Export–Import Bank, for example).

Among privately owned banks, the Bank of Tokyo is in first place in terms of total assets (Rp. 60.4 billion), closely followed by Citibank and Chase. A domestic foreign exchange bank, Pan Indonesia, is the fourth largest (Rp. 40.8 billion in assets), while the Bank of America is in fifth place. In terms of deposit holdings, Chase is first with Rp. 27.2 billion, followed by the Bangkok Bank (Rp. 21.8 billion) and Citibank (Rp. 21.4 billion). Bank of Tokyo and the above-mentioned PANIN are in fourth and fifth place, respectively. In general, it is very difficult for privately owned commercial banks to compete with the five state banks, which have an extensive network of branches and ready access to subsidized credit. The BRI has 273 branches and BNI, 214; while among privately owned banks, PANIN has 18, Bank Umum Nasional, 14, and Bank Central Asia, 12. The typical foreign-owned bank has either a single office or, at most, one other branch.

Table 8 summarizes the use of bank credit by economic sector. Unfortunately, the tale told has been heard before: in a country where the agricultural sector accounts for about three-fourths of total employment and constitutes 31 percent of GDP, bank credit is devoted mainly to other sectors. Of total bank credit—and note that more than 80 percent is granted by public-sector banks—only 7.5 percent went to agriculture. In foreign exchange credit, mining and manufacturing were the only significant recipients, often using such credit for capital-intensive, high-technology ventures. On this score, some of the ventures of PERTAMINA (a floating fertilizer plant?) are rather hard to believe.

To conclude this overview of Indonesia's financial system, a brief discussion of the 1978 devaluation seems in order. "Kenop 15," as it

TABLE 8
*Bank Credits in Rupiah and Foreign Exchange
End of 1977/78 Fiscal Year*

	Millions of Rupiahs	% total
Total	4,094,253	100.0
Agriculture	308,838	7.5
Mining*	1,044,591	25.5
Manufacturing†	1,257,550	30.7
Trade	953,140	23.2
Services	348,761	8.5
Miscellaneous	181,373	4.4
In local currency	2,979,093	72.8
Agriculture	308,516	7.5
Mining	187,778	4.6
Manufacturing	1,012,332	24.7
Trade	942,914	23.0
Services	346,789	8.5
Miscellaneous	180,764	4.4
In foreign exchange	1,115,160	27.2
Agriculture	332	neg.
Mining	856,813	20.9
Manufacturing	245,218	6.0
Trade	10,226	0.2
Services	1,972	neg.
Miscellaneous	609	neg.

*Includes credits to PERTAMINA
†Includes credits to PT Krakatau Steel
SOURCE: Bank of Indonesia, *Report for the Financial Year, 1977/78,* Table 6, p. 17. (Detail may not add to total due to rounding error.)

is widely known, involved on November 15, 1978, a 50 percent devaluation of the rupiah from the official Rp. 415=US$1 exchange rate, which had been in effect since August 1971. A plausible explanation for this action, which came at a time when the balance of payments was still in surplus and when further rises in the price of petroleum were in the offing, is that the Indonesian authorities acted to restore the purchasing power parity of the rupiah. Since 1971, Indonesia had experienced an inflation rise of some 237 percent (as measured by the Jakarta cost of living index), while the rate of inflation overseas had been much lower—export unit values of industrial countries as reported by the IMF had risen 120 percent (and exactly 100 percent for the U.S. alone). The devaluation has the potential to make a good deal of sense for Indonesia on structural grounds. To quote Howard Dick: ''The Government explained that it intended to encourage structural change which would provide a higher rate of

growth of employment by stimulating primary non-oil exports, pro-
tecting the infant manufacturing sector from import competition,
and encouraging it to develop an export orientation. It also hoped to
favour more labour-intensive methods of production by making imported capital funds and equipment more expensive."[9]

In practice, however, the market system is seldom allowed to work
in Indonesia, and this case was no exception. Businessmen attempting to raise prices of imported goods were subjected to various forms
of harrassment by the government and numerous *ad hoc* ceilings
were placed on a variety of non-traditional exports, which the devaluation was supposed to encourage. While it is too early to attempt a
comprehensive review of the consequences of this action, it seems
likely that the main results will be two. First, the rupiah will no
longer be pegged to the U.S. dollar directly; a "basket" of currencies
will be used to stabilize the exchange markets instead, very much in
line with central bank policies elsewhere. Second, government
revenues—payments by the oil companies—will rise. Those having
access to subsidized bank credit will undoubtedly continue to use
foreign exchange in much the same way as before. Indonesia still has
a long way to go in developing a functional money and capital
market.

NOTES

1. For some further detail, see Roger A. Freeman, *Socialism and Private Enterprise in Equatorial Asia,* pp. 96 ff.

2. A strident critique of the post–Sukarno period is found in Rex Mortimer (ed.),
Showcase State.

3. Robert F. Emery, *The Financial Institutions of Southeast Asia,* p. 153.

4. Ibid., p. 159. For most transactions, an exchange rate of Rp. 415 to one U.S.
dollar actually prevailed during this period.

5. H. W. Arndt, "Survey of Recent Developments," p. 21.

6. Emery, *Financial Institutions,* p. 183.

7. Howard Dick, "Survey of Recent Developments," p. 34.

8. Stephen Grenville, "Survey of Recent Developments," *Bulletin of Indonesian
Economic Studies,* March 1977, p. 28.

9. Howard Dick, "Survey of Recent Developments," p. 4.

CHAPTER 4

Malaysia

Since independence (August 1957) and the split from Singapore (August 1965), the Malaysian economy has performed extremely well, with real GNP per capita growing at about 4 percent. The development of the petroleum industry has accelerated this advance in recent years. Economic policies have stressed price stability, fiscal and monetary conservatism, and an "open" economy. Tin and rubber production for the export market continues to be very important, but non-traditional exports have been rising very rapidly.[1] In the late 1960s tin and rubber accounted for roughly one-half of export earnings, but today they total about one-third. The country's reliance on export production has exposed it to the fluctuations in demand and market prices, which characterize the world commodity market. Yet, the benefits of such exposure may have been greater than the costs. As Wolfgang Kasper has put it:

> The openness has brought advantages. It may well be that it has made possible the resilience and the adaptability of the Malaysian economy in the face of varying conditions abroad. Without economic flexibility (the result of a permanent exposure to international competition lacking in many developing countries), without easy access to foreign technology (greatly facilitated by the widespread use of high-quality English), and without access to foreign capital goods and high-quality industrial inputs from abroad, the rapid structural change during the

1960's would probably not have been possible. As we shall see in more detail later, the high degree of internal price stability in the past can also be attributed in part to the openness of the Malaysian economy.[2]

This economic setting has been most conducive to substantial financial deepening. At the time of independence, there were no indigenous, Malay-operated banks in existence, and the bulk of banking business was in the hands of foreign bank branches (there exist today five banks owned by Chinese Malaysians going back to the pre–World War II period). As recently as 1967, indigenous banks accounted for about 33 percent of total banking business.[3] As can be seen from Table 9, total financial system assets have increased almost ten-fold from 1960 to 1977. The financial assets/national income ratio shows an increase from 0.55 in 1960 to 1.28 in 1977. As pointed out in the Bank Negara Malaysia's twenty-year anniversary volume: "Studies by Goldsmith on financial structures and development have shown that in 1963, most developed economies had ratios of around 1.55, the range being 1.29 for Australia and 2.72 for Switzerland. The ratio calculated for Malaysia is in fact 'comparable' with the ratio for Australia, which had been maintained at 1.23 in 1977."[4]

Other measures of monetization and financial deepening confirm this observation that Malaysia is rapidly nearing developed countries' levels on this score. The commercial banks branching network has

TABLE 9
Malaysia's Financial System, 1960–1977
(in millions of Malaysian dollars)

	1960	1970	1977
I. Banking System	2,356(66.3%)	7,455(64.1%)	28,127(71.1%)
A. Monetary institutions	2,346(66.0%)	6,882(59.2%)	23,949(60.6%)
Central Bank	184	2,227	7,701
Currency Board	930	195	55
Commercial banks	1,232	4,460	16,193
B. Non-monetary	10(0.3%)	573(4.9%)	4,178(10.5%)
II. NBFIs*	1,197(33.7%)	4,167(35.9%)	11,417(28.9%)
A. Insurance & pension funds	836(23.5%)	3,156(27.2%)	8,161(20.6%)
Employees Provident Fund	633	2,265	5,843
B. Development finance institutions	1(0.0%)	113(1.1%)	892(2.3%)
C. Savings institutions	267(7.5%)	645(5.5%)	1,761(4.5%)
D. Other intermediaries	93(2.7%)	233(2.1%)	603(1.5%)
TOTAL	3,553(100.0%)	11,622(100.0%)	39,544(100.0%)

*Non-bank financial intermediaries
SOURCE: Bank Negara Malaysia, *Money and Banking*, p. 64.

grown to include nearly 500 branches, "giving rise to an average population to banking office ratio of 25,800, a comparatively low figure for a developing country."[5] The very rapid growth of the Malaysian commercial banking system (at an annual compound rate of more than 16 percent) tends to overshadow the considerable absolute expansion in other financial institutions as well. For example, finance companies have expanded five-fold in the 1970–1977 period, and merchant banks and discount houses have appeared on the scene.

The public sector has played a very active role in the development of financial institutions in Malaysia. The Bank Bumiputra is today the largest commercial bank with total assets of nearly M$4 billion. Two other public sector institutions are even larger, however. The first of these is the central bank, Bank Negara Malaysia, with total assets nearly twice as large as the largest commercial bank; it accounts for roughly 20 percent of total financial assets. While the bulk of the central bank's assets is held in the form of gold and foreign exchange, it does hold M$1.1 billion in government securities. The second is the Employees Provident Fund (EPF), the Malaysian equivalent of the American social security system; it holds approximately M$6 billion in total assets, with fully 95 percent of this amount being invested in government securities. Established in 1951, the EPF currently covers 73 percent of all employees in the country. Upon enactment, it covered only employees earning less than M$400 per month (raised to M$500 in 1963), but it has been extended to employees of all income levels since 1970. Since August 1975, the statutory rate of contributions has been raised from 10 percent of the employee's monthly wage, split evenly between employer and employee, to 13 percent (with 7 percent from the employer). As a result of these modifications, total contributions to the EPF have grown at an annual compound rate of 13.7 percent over the 1952–1977 period.[6] Finally, we can mention three considerably smaller institutions organized by the public sector whose main role is to provide savings facilities for the small saver and to channel funds into housing (which the EPF also does, to a considerable extent). First, the National Savings Bank/Post Office Savings Bank, with total assets of nearly M$1 billion, is quite active in rural areas. Second, the two housing societies, Borneo Housing Mortgage Finance (operating in Sabah and Sarawak) and the Malaysia Building Society Berhad, resemble publicly sponsored savings and loan associations in that they provide funds for low-cost housing. Therefore, all in all, public sector entities in Malaysia by now add up

TABLE 10

Domestic Banks in Malaysia, 1977

(in millions of Malaysian dollars)

Bank (no. of branches)	Total Assets	Deposits	Net Worth
1. Bank Bumiputra (52)	3,780.4	2,965.8	117.8
2. Malayan Banking* (110)	3,433.3	2,602.4	203.3
3. UMBC* (39)	1,730.6	1,241.7	70.8
4. United Asian Bank (28)	1,195.4	674.8	34.1
5. Public (11)	315.2	212.9	22.4
6. Perwira Habib (14)	269.2	199.5	5.0
7. Hock Hua (Sarawak) (5)	223.6	154.8	12.4
8. D & C (9)	207.1	126.4	24.7
9. Kwong Yik* (7)	201.0	170.8	17.5
10. Southern Banking (7)	151.0	86.8	13.3
11. Bank Buruh* (1)	115.5	96.4	7.8
12. Bank Hin Lee (5)	112.1	74.3	13.8
13. Kwong Lee (4)	110.1	80.9	10.9
14. Oriental (8)	108.1	90.9	2.3
15. Hock Hua (Sabah) (3)	104.7	67.3	5.7
16. Kong Ming (4)	76.2	38.1	5.3
17. Pacific (2)	67.4	51.1	9.8
18. Wah Tat (2)	46.7	30.7	3.2
19. Bian Chang (1)	34.3	25.9	5.3
20. Bank Utama* (1)	9.3	4.2	4.9
TOTAL (313)	12,291.2	8,995.7	590.3

*Year ending June 30

SOURCE: The SGV Group, *A Study of Commercial Banks in Malaysia, 1977*, pp. 11–12.

to a total roughly equal to privately owned intermediaries; yet, these governmental institutions have been devoid of the sort of corruption and mismanagement that seems to accompany the placement of public funds in a number of other countries in the region.

Turning now to the structure of commercial banking in Malaysia, Table 10 lists the twenty indigenous commercial banks operating as of the end of 1977 (Bank Utama commenced operations during 1977), with total assets of M$12.3 billion. Prior to 1976, foreign-owned commercial banks accounted for more than half of total banking system assets; but at the end of 1977, the indigenous banks forged ahead decisively with a 57 percent share.[7] At the end of 1959, the five largest banks in Malaysia were all foreign-incorporated and they accounted for about 72 percent of total bank resources. At the end of 1978, three of the largest five were locally incorporated institutions. The extent of concentration had also lessened; the five largest banks account for only 57 percent of total bank resources, 61 percent of total deposits, and 56 percent of total bank loans and advances. The branching network also appears to have become more competitive: the top five banks accounted for 65 percent of the total number of bank offices in the country in 1959, when there were only 26 such offices. Today, the number of branches is around 500, and the top five banking organizations cover 58 percent of these.[8]

The foreign banks shown in Table 11 continue to play an important role in the financial markets, though the relative importance of that role is likely to continue to diminish. The top two foreign banks, Chartered ($2.3 billion ringgits) and HSBC ($1.7 billion), are of British origin while the next two are headquartered in Singapore—suggesting that close economic ties have continued between Malaysia and Singapore after their political separation. Two large Asian banks, the Bank of Tokyo and the Bangkok Bank, occupy the fifth and eighth spots respectively. American banks are represented by Citibank, Bank of America, and Chase. Three other U.S. banks, Manufacturers Hanover, Morgan Guaranty, and Seattle First, have recently established representative offices there.

The conclusion that emerges from this discussion is rather obvious. Malaysia has been immensely successful in mobilizing funds through

TABLE 11

Branches of Foreign Banks in Malaysia, 1977
(in millions of Malaysian dollars)

Bank (no. of branches)	Total Assets	Deposits
1. Chartered (35)	2,336.7	1,704.8
2. Hongkong and Shanghai (36)	1,718.5	1,264.5
3. Overseas-Chinese (25)	1,116.1	976.0
4. Chung Kiaw (16)	707.9	433.4
5. Tokyo* (1)	686.9	157.2
6. Citibank* (3)	643.4	253.8
7. Overseas Union Union (12)	406.6	282.2
8. Bangkok (1)	329.3	110.3
9. Bank of America (1)	322.5	124.6
10. L'Indochine (2)	267.9	116.0
11. Lee Wah (9)	252.1	203.0
12. Chase (1)	248.4	80.8
13. Algemene (2)	201.9	44.5
14. European Asian (1)	188.4	66.0
15. Canton (1)	59.0	36.0
16. Nova Scotia* (1)	53.0	20.8
17. United Overseas (1)	26.9	18.8
TOTAL (148)	9,565.5	5,892.7

*Bank of Tokyo, March 31; Citibank, December 20; Nova Scotia, October 31.
SOURCE: The SGV Group, *A Study of Commercial Banks in Malaysia, 1977*, pp. 11–12.

financial intermediaries. The banking system has played a very important role, and monetization and the "banking habit" seem very well developed.[9] Whether such financial deepening has promoted economic growth and development is a more difficult question; in other words, has the allocation process been optimal? It is very difficult to develop a single criterion of optimality, of course. From an individual banker's point of view, it may be defined in terms of maximizing profit and minimizing risk. An economist may think in terms of contributions made to long-term growth, employment effects, and income distribution; while a politician would ideally be aware of all of these, as well as of regional, racial, and public relations aspects of the credit allocation process. The policy-maker charged with the operating responsibility for somehow reconciling all of these perceptions of optimality certainly has a complex and often thankless task.[10]

Table 12 summarizes the direction of commercial bank lending in Malaysia. Generally, the banking system in the early 1960s was en-

TABLE 12
Direction of Commercial Bank Lending in Malaysia, 1960–1978
(in millions of Malaysian dollars)

	1960	1970	1978*
Agriculture	37.0	240.3	829.5
Rubber	35.0	114.5	145.4
Palm oil	0.3	35.0	140.8
Forestry	0.3	62.7	325.9
Mining and quarrying	8.2	51.2	106.4
Manufacturing	53.2	465.6	1,999.0
Rubber products	22.4	41.7	95.7
Rice milling	11.1	27.2	27.8
Food and tobacco	4.1	40.7	157.1
Textiles and clothing	0.8	12.2	108.7
Metal products	2.0	99.5	323.4
Building materials	1.3	39.9	172.0
Real estate and construction	19.1	206.5	1,302.3
General commerce	168.2	471.9	1,768.9
Professionals and individuals	94.6	376.9	2,187.0
Business purposes	n.a.	155.0	626.8
Housing	n.a.	n.a.	1,160.5
Other	n.a.	221.9	399.7
Miscellaneous	83.2	258.2	1,461.2
Domestic trade bills	10.8	118.1	990.1
Foreign trade bills	36.0	166.0	547.5
Lending to public sector	0.1	4.9	581.8
TOTAL	510.4	2,359.6	11,773.7

* As of the end of September 1978
SOURCE: Bank Negara Malaysia, *Money and Banking*, p. 158.

gaged largely in financing commerce, and credit was usually quite short-term and self-liquidating in nature. Loans to agriculture amounted to only 7.2 percent of total credit outstanding, primarily to rubber plantations, and credit to the manufacturing sector was 10.4 percent of the total. By 1978, bank credit reflects the rapid industrialization and diversification taking place in Malaysia. The manufacturing sector currently accounts for 17 percent of commercial bank credit, having surpassed commerce as the most important user of bank funds. In relative terms, the most rapid increase has taken place in bank lending for real estate, construction, and housing, which has risen from 3.7 percent in 1960 to 11.1 percent of total bank credit in 1978. On the other hand, agricultural credit has declined slightly as has credit to the mining and quarrying sector, although it can be pointed out that credit to non-traditional borrowers in the agricultural sector, particularly palm oil and forestry products, has risen sharply. This fact may indicate that commercial bankers are willing to search out profitable opportunities in rural areas— perhaps credit is available to traditional agriculture from other sources. Yet, to some extent, Lee Hock Lock's assessment of the banking system still rings true:

> A shortcoming of the Malaysian banking system is that banking activities have continued for the most part along traditional lines and are not fully in keeping with the development needs of the country. Loans and advances have, by and large, been of a short-term character. On the direction of lending, a large share has gone to the financing of commerce and the activities of professional and private individuals although the share going to manufacturing has increased. Half of the bank lending to professional and private individuals was for private purposes (this is even more true today, if we classify housing as a private use of funds— GJV). As noted earlier, loans to manufacturing were largely for the manufacture of rubber products and rice milling in the past but a more diversified pattern has emerged recently. Loans to agriculture were mainly to the rubber industry. Bank investments in government securities have mainly been of short maturities and subscriptions to longer term government securities are still small. . . .[11]

No assessment of the Malaysian economy during the past twenty years or so can be complete without bringing up, at least briefly, the overriding question of race. After the May 1969 race riots, the government announced a "New Economic Policy," aimed at greatly increasing Malay participation in the economy; for example, a deliberate "bumiputraization" of all business ownership. This was to be achieved not by a disruptive redistribution of assets, but rather by increasing active participation of Malays in all additions to the stock of wealth. This principle was further elaborated by the Third Malaysia Plan, 1976–1980, which set up a two-pronged attack: (1) "to eradicate poverty among all Malaysians" by 1990, or thereabouts (78 percent of all poverty households are Malay, but only 13 percent Chinese), and (2) "to restructure Malaysian society so that identification of race with economic function and geographical location is reduced and eventually eliminated." Government planning documents indicate certain quantitative goals for total asset ownership by 1990. The Malay share is expected to rise from an initial level of 2.4 percent in 1970 to 30 percent two decades later; the indigenous non-Malay share is intended to reach 40 percent, up slightly from 34 percent in 1970. This implies a sharp reduction in foreign equity—from 63 percent in 1970 to only 30 percent in 1990. Just to what extent the financial system will be regulated in this wealth transfer is unclear at present, but the Malaysian authorities should be aware of great hazards in that connection. Hainsworth reports that

> scandals are already beginning to break in connection with transfer of equity holdings, and it is hard to see how corruption and mismanagement can be avoided when such lucrative "unearned" spoils are there for the more well-placed and avaricious among the elite to contend for. To foreign business, such enforced equity participation along with the extensive controls and oversight envisaged in the new Industrial Coordination Act (ICA) appear as further ingenious tithing of their operations (on top of the salaried Malay directors and often-under-utilized managers and consultants they have been obliged to employ). Along with reservation of broader ranges of activity for Malay-only enterprises, this could seriously discourage continuing foreign investment in Malaysia and disrupt modern sector development in general.[12]

NOTES

1. For further details on the costs and benefits of the diversification strategy, see David Lim, *Economic Growth and Development in West Malaysia, 1947–1970.*

2. Wolfgang Kasper, *Malaysia: A Study in Successful Economic Development.* There is considerable disagreement in the professional literature about whether commodity price fluctuations adversely affect economic growth. Since the marginal propensity to save out of transitory income is likely to be higher than the MPS for permanent income, foreign exchange windfalls are likely to aid capital formation, when

prices are on the upswing. See P. A. Yotopoulos and J. B. Nugent, *The Economics of Development*, Chapter 18.

3. See Robert F. Emery, *The Financial Institutions of Southeast Asia*, pp. 271–272.

4. Bank Negara Malaysia (Economics Research and Statistics Department), *Money and Banking in Malaysia, 1959-1979*, p. 82.

5. Ibid., p. 65.

6. Ibid., pp. 228–230.

7. It should be pointed out that Table 9 gives total banking system assets as M$16.2 billion, while Table 10 and Table 11 add up to more than M$21 billion for the same date. The probable explanation of this discrepancy lies in the inter-bank loan market, since the central bank apparently defines asset size on a net basis while the SGV group uses balance sheet data.

8. Bank Negara Malaysia, *Money and Banking*, pp. 142–145.

9. Richard C. Porter, ''The Promotion of the 'Banking Habit' and Economic Development,'' pp. 346–366.

10. A good discussion of the issues raised above is found in E. K. Fisk, ''The Justification and Assessment of Small Loans by Development Banking Institutions,'' pp. 1–11. In *Malayan Economic Review*, which discusses the development finance system of Papua New Guinea but also makes reference to Malaysian experience.

11. Lee Hock Lock, *Household Saving in West Malaysia and the Problem of Financing Economic Development*, p. 177.

12. Geoffrey B. Hainsworth, ''Economic Growth and Poverty in Southeast Asia,'' pp. 14–17.

CHAPTER 5
The Philippines

In terms of the sheer number of financial institutions, as well as in the richness of various institutional arrangements for mobilizing and allocating funds, the Philippines is probably in the forefront of the ASEAN region. Table 13 summarizes the asset holdings of the various component parts of the Philippines' financial system. It can be seen that the monetary institutions—the central bank and deposit banks—account for 64 percent of total financial assets. In the nonmonetary part of the financial system, various public sector intermediaries play a very significant role. The largest of these is the Development Bank of the Philippines, which was established in 1958 to take over the functions of the Rehabilitation Finance Corporation. It currently has total assets in excess of P18 billion and operates 41 branches, 8 sub-branches, and 10 agencies. While the bulk of its paid-in capital was provided by the government, and government agencies provide a large part of its deposit base currently, it can accept deposits from the public and it also raises capital by issuing bonds. The Government Service Insurance System (GSIS), with total assets of approximately P8 billion, was founded in 1937, and is currently the largest non-bank financial institution in the Philippines. It provides retirement annuities, insurance, and other services to government employees, for whom enrollment is mandatory. The GSIS offers real estate and salary and policy loans to its members, but it

TABLE 13
Assets of Philippine Financial Institutions, December 31, 1978
(in millions of pesos)

	Levels	Per Cent	Distribution
Financial System	197,077.7	100.0	
I. Monetary System	125,792.8	63.8	100.0
A. Monetary authorities	35,180.9	17.8	28.0
B. Deposit money banks	90,611.9	46.0	72.0
1. Commercial banks	89,798.6	45.6	71.4
2. Rural banks with demand deposits	813.3	0.4	0.6
II. Non-Monetary Financial System	71,284.9	36.2	100.0
A. Bank institutions	30,627.8	15.6	43.0
1. Thrift banks	5,602.8	2.9	7.9
a. Savings banks	3,896.8	2.0	5.5
b. Private development banks	759.7	0.4	1.1
c. Stock savings & loan assns.	946.3	0.5	1.3
2. Rural banks–non-d/d	3,298.7	1.7	4.6
3. Specialized banks	21,726.3	11.0	30.5
a. Development Bank of the Phil.	18,209.7	9.2	25.6
b. Land bank	3,446.1	1.7	4.8
c. Philippine Amanah Bank	70.5	0.1	0.1
B. Non-bank financial institutions	40,657.1	20.6	57.0
1. Investment houses	4,762.5	2.4	6.7
2. Finance companies	7,365.7	3.7	10.3
3. Investment companies	4,651.1	2.4	6.5
4. Securities dealers/brokers	1,119.8	0.6	1.6
5. Pawnshops	192.3	0.1	0.3
6. Fund managers	834.4	0.4	1.2
7. Lending investors	18.5	—	—
8. Non-stock savings & loan assns.	191.8	0.1	0.3
9. Mutual bldg. & loan assn.	21.4	—	—
10. Private investment companies	6,167.5*	3.1	8.6
11. Specialized non-bank	15,332.1	7.8	21.5
a. GSIS	7,833.3	4.0	11.0
b. SSS	6,032.8	3.1	8.5
c. ACA	427.8	0.2	0.6
d. NIDC	1,038.2	0.5	1.4

*As of December 31, 1977
SOURCE: Central Bank of the Philippines.

also has substantial investments in stocks and bonds. The Social
Security System (SSS) was set up in 1954, but did not commence operations until 1958, due to opposition from management and labor.
The system does not cover the agricultural labor force and most service workers. Its P6 billion in assets is invested in real estate finance
and government securities. The National Investment and Development Corporation (NIDC), the Land Bank, and a couple of smaller
organizations round out the list of government-sponsored financial
institutions. Adding in the Philippines National Bank and the Phil-

ippines Veterans Bank, with a total of P25.1 in assets, we get a total of about P97 billion; roughly one-half of the total flow of funds comes from the public sector.

As is usually the case, commercial banks are predominant among private institutions. Table 14 provides a listing of these banks, grouped by total assets, deposits, and net worth. The domination of the banking system by the government-owned [Philippine] National Bank is quite clear-cut: the PNB is three times as large as Citibank,

TABLE 14
Commercial Banks in the Philippines, 1978
(in millions of pesos)

Bank (no. of branches)	Assets	Deposits	Net Worth
A. Government	25,153.2	10,468.1	1,979.4
Philippines National (186)	23,327.0	9,153.5	1,810.9
Veterans (26)	1,826.2	1,314.6	168.5
B. Foreign	11,111.7	2,482.1	7,465.0
Citibank (3)	7,079.9	1,148.8	100.0
Bank of America (1)	2,272.2	628.7	—
Hongkong and Shanghai (2)	1,023.7	373.8	131.9
Chartered (3)	735.9	330.8	139.6
C. Private Domestic	55,260.6	31,888.8	5,114.1
Bank of Philippine Islands (78)	4,442.0	3,001.3	400.7
Metrobank (112)	4,072.7	2,616.1	235.0
Allied (39)	3,709.3	1,725.3	276.9
United Coconut (37)	3,436.9	2,733.6	327.0
Commercial and Industrial (75)	3,236.4	2,142.3	238.7
Far East (40)	3,202.3	1,889.6	257.4
Rizal (34)	3,092.3	1,517.3	201.0
China (19)	2,814.8	1,317.9	288.6
Pacific (36)	2,544.4	1,351.8	171.7
Solidbank (40)	2,524.2	1,778.1	266.1
Equitable (35)	2,443.6	1,460.5	267.8
Manilabank (46)	2,206.9	1,261.6	197.6
Comtrust (49)	1,973.4	1,257.1	172.6
Philbanking (41)	1,952.6	910.0	158.3
Insular (48)	1,814.4	878.4	202.8
Traders (29)	1,801.8	1,293.9	138.0
Prudential (42)	1,603.8	1,089.7	177.2
Communications (49)	1,410.3	575.7	186.1
Security (32)	1,369.4	710.3	159.0
Associated Citizens (32)	1,110.3	504.4	135.4
Interbank (10)	976.3	231.6	112.1
City Trust (19)	842.2	369.6	127.8
Republic (46)	745.4	313.6	92.4
Filman (21)	709.7	383.3	92.3
Producers (17)	682.1	264.6	135.3
Phil. Trust (10)	561.1	311.2	136.3

SOURCE: The SGV Group, *A Study of Commercial Banks in the Philippines, 1978.*

which started operations in that country in 1902, and roughly five times as large as the privately owned Bank of the Philippine Islands, whose history goes back to 1851. Both Hongkong and Shanghai Banking Corporation (1875) and Chartered (1873) have recently celebrated centennials of bank operations. Based on return on net worth, the most profitable five banks are: United Coconut (a 37.2 percent net earnings as a percent of average net worth), Allied (22.6 percent), China (20.1 percent), Metrobank (20.1 percent), and Far East Banking and Trust (19.3 percent). Bank credit allocation on a sector-by-sector basis shows a picture rather similar to that found in other ASEAN countries. The bulk of commercial bank credit was devoted to manufacturing (about 32 percent) and trade (29 percent). Agriculture, with 10.6 percent, was a distant third, although it is true that the Philippines has a number of specialized institutions designed to provide agricultural credit.[1] In particular, we should mention the existence of more than 900 separate rural banks, although overall assets for this type of institution only total about P4 billion.[2] Nevertheless, the World Bank reports that "the share of credit to agriculture declined steadily from 40 percent in the early 1960's and 7 percent in 1973, while the shares of credit to the manufacturing and trade sectors rose, partly because of the increased importance of industry in the economy."[3]

In the early 1970s, a sharp increase in nominal interest rates took place: interest rates on savings and time deposits, which had ranged from 5 to 9.5 percent, were increased to a range of 6 to 11.5 percent. Administrative ceilings were lifted on time deposits having a maturity of over two years, and savings banks offered rates averaging 14.5 percent on these. Nevertheless, the inflation rate accelerated even more, and real yields turned more negative than they had been at any time in the 1950s or 1960s. The World Bank reports a yield of −20.4 percent on savings deposits, −17.6 percent on time deposits, and −12.7 percent on government securities. As a result, "unregulated money-market rates had risen in some instances to levels well above 30 percent on an annual basis in 1973 and 1974, and the growth of these latter instruments exceeded that of traditional deposits. Total short-term deposit substitutes outstanding, which had amounted to 24 percent of total medium- and long-term time and savings deposits in commercial banks and thrift institutions at the end of 1972, were equal to 82 percent at the end of 1974."[4] Because of a depreciating peso in the 1970s and a concern for the political situation and inflationary pressure, considerable divestment of foreign capital has been taking place in the Philippine economy. Withdrawal of foreign investment rose from about US$8 million in the first half of 1977 to about US$12 million during the same period in 1978. The banking system was also affected by this development: the Bank of America decided to withdraw from its minority participation in the Insular Bank of Asia and America, following the lead of Irving Trust and Grindlays National Bank of London (from the Philippine Bank of Communications and Genbank, respectively); Canadian Royal Bank withdrew from Traders. The Far Eastern Economic Review points out that

> in no other sector of the Philippine economy has change been as frequent as in banking. Two ailing ones were restored to financial health, but under new names, owners and managers practically handpicked by the Central Bank. They are Genbank, now Allied Banking Corporation, and the former Continental Bank and Trust Company, now International Corporate Bank. Majority ownership in Filipinas Manufacturers changed hands, but it retained its corporate name. What used to be Feati Bank and Trust Company became City Trust Banking Corporation. Following a substantial equity transfer to sugar planter-buyers, Republic Bank was abandoned in favour of Republic Planters Bank. The Catholic Church sold a portion of its majority holdings in Philippine Trust Company.[5]

It should be pointed out that Central Bank policies had to be carried out in a difficult institutional and political framework. Strong sentiment will always be present in favor of low interest rates and an overvalued exchange rate. In the case of the Philippines, such desires were probably strengthened by a number of special factors. In connection with interest rates, the Catholic scholastics have invariably adopted a strong anti-usury position (reflected in the Anti-Usury Law of 1916), imposing limits of 12 and 14 percent, respectively, on secured and unsecured bank loans. In these inflationary times, one would hope that doctrine on this could be modified to introduce the concept of the real rate of interest—for example, the nominal interest rate minus the inflation rate. On foreign exchange valuation, the politically powerful elite was vitally interested in the cost of luxury consumer goods, virtually all imported, as well as foreign travel and education (an American college degree being highly prized). More specifically, the Central Bank was often assigned responsibility for much more than its traditional role of safeguarding bank soundness and monetary stability. As aptly summarized by Roman A. Cruz, Jr., then Undersecretary of the Department of Finance:

> It has had to compensate for the absence of an effective economic planning machinery in the government, for the failure of Congress to revise the antiquated tax and tariff laws of the country in the interest of sound development, and for the tendencies of an impatient government to incur expenditures beyond what can be financed by tax revenues and by borrowing from a yet limited money and capital market. . . . From the middle of the 1950's on, it has had to compensate for the revenue shortfalls of an inadequate tax system by absorbing government debt instruments into its portfolio to finance budgetary deficits.[6]

The assessment of the inadequacies of the financial structure provided by Robert F. Emery still seems to apply. Existing financial institutions in the Philippines serve certain sectors of the economy quite well, notably "trade and commerce, agricultural-processing facilities, and the working-capital needs of tne well-established corporations." On the other hand, tenant farmers and small-scale industrial activities ("home and cottage industries") find it quite difficult to gain access to loans. Many corporations are said to be "undercapitalized," and consumers lack adequate credit facilities.[7] This is certainly not due to a lack of specialized institutions. As noted earlier, the Philippines has an unusually large variety of financial institutions, and organizations with the words "development," "land," and "agricultural" in their titles abound. This fact was also recognized by the World Bank:

> Because of its extensive influence over the financial system, the government will need to take the initiative by encouraging financial institutions to lengthen their maturities . . . and by improving credit delivery, especially to agriculture and to small- and medium-scale industries. Improving the operating efficiency of financial institutions should lead to reduced spreads and lower costs. The growth of financial intermediaries in the Philippines has been quite extensive but uneven. Consequently, although there is no need to establish whole new classes of institutions, the less developed ones, such as savings and mortgage

banks and the securities markets, should be given sufficient incentives to grow.[8]

While it may have been difficult for the World Bank to spell out fully the implications of such government initiatives, these may involve a greater reliance on competition and market allocation than has been the case in the past. The Philippines appears to have an ample supply of indigenous entrepreneurial talent, a hard-working labor force, and a strong tradition of educational aspirations. One suspects that, on balance, the government's intervention in the economic process has had almost as significant negative consequences as positive ones. Baldwin concludes in his comprehensive study of trade policy in the Philippines that

> the main driving forces for sustaining development will have to come from the internal economic interactions among the various sectors. The foreign sector can play an important role in facilitating this growth, but the easy days of import substitution are over. Moreover, trying to force the domestic production of manufactured intermediates and capital goods in the manner used to achieve local production of simply processed consumer goods is likely to prove self-defeating because of the greater import requirements of the former and the adverse effect on exports. . . . Yet, no change in development policies will prevent periodic economic crises unless the government exercises a much greater degree of fiscal and monetary discipline.[9]

NOTES

1. See Table 6 in Central Bank of the Philippines, *Thirtieth Annual Report, 1978,* p. 15.

2. For more detail on the history of the rural banks system, which was established in 1952 largely under the leadership of the Central Bank of the Philippines, see Robert F. Emery, *The Financial Institutions of Southeast Asia,* pp. 398–403.

3. International Bank for Reconstruction and Development, *The Philippines: Priorities and Prospects for Development,* p. 359.

4. Ibid., pp. 358–359.

5. Far Eastern Economic Review, *Asia Yearbook, 1979,* p. 286.

6. Roman A. Cruz, Jr., "Monetary Policy and Economic Development," p. 241.

7. Robert F. Emery, *The Financial Institutions of Southeast Asia,* p. 479.

8. International Bank for Reconstruction and Development, *The Philippines: Priorities and Prospects for Development,* p. 380.

9. Robert E. Baldwin, *The Philippines: Foreign Trade Regimes and Economic Development,* p. 152.

CHAPTER 6

Singapore

As already noted, Singapore has become a significant international financial center in recent years: the banking system has benefitted from substantial liberalization of rules and regulations; the concentration ratios are quite low; and the competitive market situation has kept interest rates and the foreign exchange rate quite stable. In large part, the very rapid growth in financial transactions taking place in Singapore probably reflects the fact that the other ASEAN capitals, indeed most other potential locations for a regional financial center, restrict banking transactions to a greater or lesser extent. This development of ''off-shore banking'' in Singapore seems to parallel trends elsewhere in the world, and is a good example of the sort of market fragmentation discussed in the introductory section. For instance, London's well-known Eurodollar market appears to have sprung up partly in response to regulations governing East–West trade, and partly in response to Federal Reserve rules governing foreign lending by the head offices of U.S. banks. Also, in many, if not most, ASEAN countries direct private foreign investment—i.e., equity participation by non-national interests (sometimes defined to include indigenous investors belonging to minority groups)—has been subject to a great deal of scrutiny and restraint. In other words, foreign-owned capital has been deliberately differentiated from locally controlled funds, thus leading to yet another type of market fragmentation. Broadly speaking, the Singapore financial market performs an intermediary function, which greatly reduces such fragmentation. Apparently radical political opinion in Asian countries views borrowing in the "Asian Currency Market" in Singapore very differently from allowing "American bankers" and "Arab investors" direct access to the domestic money and capital markets in such nations.

The commercial banking system in Singapore is well-established and the banking habit seems to be quite strong. A number of foreign banks can trace their history to the second half of the nineteenth century, and the separation of Singapore from Malaysia (August 1965) was handled quite smoothly insofar as the banking system is concerned.[1] Today several Singapore banks operate a net of branches in Malaysia and the reverse is true as well. Table 15 shows the assets, deposits, and net worth of twelve Singaporean domestic banks. As noted earlier, the largest commercial bank is the government-sponsored Development Bank of Singapore, established in July 1968; but the DBS does not dominate the system as a whole, as has often been the case among developing countries. In fact, the two largest private banks are somewhat understated in terms of asset size by the data used in this table. The United Overseas Bank, Ltd. (UOB), also owns 82.6 percent of Chung Kiaw, the fourth largest private bank, and

TABLE 15
Domestic Banks in Singapore, 1977
(in millions of Singapore dollars)

Bank (no. of branches)	Assets	Deposits	Net Worth
*Development Bank of Singapore (12)	3,391.8	1,200.5	147.8
*United-Overseas (26)	2,990.3	1,577.6	332.4
*Overseas-Chinese (18)	2,055.7	1,539.6	311.8
*Overseas Union (26)	1,767.2	1,208.7	121.6
Chung Kiaw (16)	644.6	540.1	67.7
Asia Commercial (5)	542.0	233.5	57.4
*Tat Lee (5)	381.9	189.8	43.9
Far Eastern (4)	350.7	226.4	17.8
Industrial & Commercial (7)	298.1	179.9	21.3
Four Seas (4)	276.4	186.7	44.0
*International Bank of Singapore (1)	240.9	137.6	26.8
*Lee Wah (4)	128.8	81.7	19.2
Bank of Singapore (3)	73.7	46.8	17.1
TOTAL	13,142.1	7,348.9	1,228.8

* Accept off-shore deposits
SOURCE: The SGV Group, *A Study of Commercial Banks in Singapore, 1977.*

100 percent of the capital stock of Lee Wah. Similarly, the Overseas–Chinese Banking Corporation (OCBC) owns 99 percent of Four Seas Communications Bank, Ltd., the oldest local bank (going back to 1906) and 88 percent of the fledgling Bank of Singapore.[2] Furthermore, the largest three private banks overshadow the Development Bank of Singapore in deposit size, and UOB and OCBC have a much stronger net worth position. All of the four largest private banks have very sizeable branch networks. Seven of the twelve local banks covered by Table 15 also engage in the business of off-shore banking, the so-called Asian Dollar Market.[3]

The off-shore banking business in Singapore dates back only to 1968, when the Bank of America asked the government's permission to establish "a separate offshore dollar unit in its corporate finance division, which would borrow non-resident foreign currency and lend it elsewhere." Permission was granted on October 1, when "the unit was authorized to start operations with a $200,000 deposit base." A year later, five additional commercial banks followed suit: Citibank, locally owned OCBC, Chartered, the United Chase Merchants Bank, and the Hongkong and Shanghai Banking Corporation.[4] The impetus for the development of this market came partly because of the time difference between Singapore and the world money markets—trading markets—trading can be taking place there, while the rest of the world is closed. However, Singapore was chosen above Hongkong and Tokyo due to tax and regulatory considerations. Singapore was willing not to tax interest earned on non-resident accounts, while Hongkong has a 15 percent withholding tax. On the other hand, Singapore does tax income derived from foreign currency lending (at 40 percent prior to August 1973, but at 10 percent since that date). Thus, as Zoran Hodjera points out: "It is, therefore, in the interest of foreign banks having branches in both financial centers to maximize earnings from deposits in Singapore and earnings from offshore lending in Hongkong."[5] Currently, it is more proper to speak of offshore banking in both cities as the Asian Currency Market, but Hodjera estimates that 92 to 95 percent of total assets and liabilities has been denominated in U.S. dollars. This is partly due to the fact that nearly half of all syndicated credit is arranged and taken up by American banks and partly due to the traditional role of the U.S. dollar as the principal "vehicle currency."[6]

The number of banks participating in the Asian Dollar Market has grown from 11 at the end of 1969 to about 70 at present; the size of the market grew from $123 million in 1969 to US$17 billion at the end of 1976, "which amounted to an average annual growth rate of 75 per cent, two and a half times the average growth rate of the Euro-currency market."[7] Over this period, the separation between resident and non-resident banking has become less clear-cut, with an easing of regulations by the Singaporean government. Since July 1978, "the sole limitation now is that an offshore bank's loans to Singapore residents must not exceed a total of S$30 million, an amount believed to be double the previous restriction. While some off-shore banks, long conditioned to ignoring the domestic market, have suggested that it will take time to adjust to the new regulations, there is little doubt that [the residents] almost all welcome the opportunities offered by them, and that as a consequence Singapore's standing as an international banking centre has been enhanced."[8] There are, as of the end of 1977, 37 foreign commercial banks operating in Singapore, with either a full or restricted license, having assets of S$44.3 billion. In addition, 25 purely off-shore banks hold nearly S$20 billion in assets. Combining the largest banks in both groups, we derive the list of 25 largest foreign banks given in Table 16, which reads like a veritable "Who's Who" of multinational banking. The First National City Bank, which has been in Singapore since 1902, is the largest commercial bank in terms of asset size. However, it is being challenged for that position by the Bank of America, which is in first place when measured by size of deposits. Interestingly, third place is occupied by the Soviet Union's Moscow Narodny Bank, which also is active in Hongkong and is sometimes cited as having founded the Eurodollar market. It is rumored in banking circles that Moscow Narodny has made some very poor business deals in the Far East, and that it remains prominent at quite a substantial cost to the Soviet taxpayer. Nine of the largest 25 banking institutions in Singapore are listed by virtue of their off-shore business only; rather few foreign banks possess a branch network—the Malayan Banking Berhad has 22; Chartered, 20; Hongkong and Shanghai, 10; and UMBC, 7. The Bank of America and the Bank of China have 4 apiece, while Chase and Citibank have 3 each.

Relative to the Eurocurrency market, with total assets of roughly $900 billion or more, the Asian Currency Market is still relatively small. Total assets at the end of 1978 are estimated in the $25 to $30 billion range. However, it performs a number of important functions in the region and for world financial markets. The market provides

TABLE 16
Principal Foreign Banks in Singapore, 1977
(in millions of Singapore dollars)

Bank	Assets	Deposits
Citibank	5,628.2	2,833.7
Bank of America	5,315.3	4,110.4
Moscow Narodny	5,175.6	1,719.4
Chase	3,213.1	713.3
Chartered	2,507.9	1,947.4
Banque Nationale de Paris	2,463.3	1,450.9
Tokyo	2,039.2	888.2
First of Chicago	1,789.1	540.2
Bankers Trust*	1,714.7	903.9
European Asian	1,698.4	563.8
National Westminster*	1,661.9	342.2
Swiss Bank*	1,442.3	464.8
Hongkong and Shanghai	1,387.5	862.2
Credit Suisse	1,292.3	969.7
Chemical*	1,243.9	1,033.2
American Express	1,222.5	694.9
Dresdner	1,216.4	934.2
Morgan Guaranty*	1,094.4	1,037.3
Banca Commerciale	1,088.7	194.8
Manufacturers Hanover*	1,054.8	777.0
Montreal*	1,046.6	969.5
Toronto-Dominion	1,039.1	653.6
Indosuez	1,038.2	640.0
Republic of Dallas*	974.4	701.4
Mitsubishi	893.0	536.4
TOTAL	63,895.5	36,768.7

*Offshore banks; not all fiscal years end 12/31
SOURCE: The SGV Group, *A Study of Commercial Banks in Singapore, 1977.*

for around-the-clock arbitrage, and has been an important source of funds for other ASEAN countries. It has provided a channel for the recycling of funds owned by the petroleum-exporting countries, and it has begun to provide some "maturity transformation" (by borrowing short and lending long). Hodjera estimates that Singapore's GNP is only about 1 percent higher than it would be in the absence of the Asian Currency Market, a rather modest amount, but its impact on Singapore's income and employment seems likely to grow.

NOTES

1. For further detail, see P. J. Drake, *Financial Development in Malaya and Singapore,* especially Chapter 6.
2. The SGV Group, *A Study of Commercial Banks in Singapore, 1977.*

3. For a good discussion of its development, see Anindya K. Bhattacharya, *The Asian Dollar Market: International Offshore Financing* (New York: Praeger Publishers, 197.)

4. Ibid., p. 6.

5. "The Asian Currency Market: Singapore as a Regional Financial Center," *International Monetary Fund Staff Papers,* June 1978, p. 226.

6. Ibid., p. 231.

7. Ibid., p. 226.

8. Far Eastern Economic Review, *Asia Yearbook, 1979,* p. 293.

CHAPTER 7

Thailand

The financial system of Thailand is essentially controlled by its domestic commercial banks, most with a long history of operations. However, in recent years, finance companies have become a more significant source of medium-term business and consumer credit and were competing quite effectively for consumer-size promissory notes, essentially having the same characteristics as time deposits (especially before the Ministry of Finance and the Bank of Thailand raised the minimum amount of such accounts).[1] Table 17 lists the 16 domestically chartered commercial banks operating in the kingdom at the end of 1978. In the case of Thailand, it is possible to draw on Rozental's pioneering study for data on commercial bank operations and to present some comparable statistics for the early 1960s.[2] It can be seen that total commercial bank assets have grown at an annual compound rate of 22.5 percent over the 1962–1978 period, indicating that monetization and financial deepening are proceeding quite well. Despite this rapid expansion in the banking system, the currency ratio (currency held by the public divided by the total money supply) remains quite high, fluctuating between 60 and 66 percent during the past ten years. The commercial banks' network of branch offices has been a major source of growth; currently, more than 1,300 branches are in operation. While fully 40 percent of these are located in the wealthy

TABLE 17
Domestic Banks in Thailand, 1962–78
(in millions of baht)

Bank (no. of offices)	1962	1978	Growth Rate
Bangkok (204)	2,374	88,791	25.4%
Krung Thai (161)*	2,048	31,040	18.6%
Farmers (193)	472	24,963	28.3%
Commercial (98)	605	14,615	22.0%
Ayudhya (125)	567	13,536	21.9%
Metropolitan (52)	544	11,164	20.7%
City (97)	397	8,889	21.4%
Commerce (116)	525	8,177	18.8%
First Bangkok (49)†	290	8,161	23.3%
Military (55)	288	6,108	21.1%
Trust (24)‡	n.a.	5,030	`n.a.
Asia (22)	327	4,868	18.4%
Union (61)	313	4,233	17.7%
Danu (14)	182	2,269	17.1%
Laem Thong (3)	244	1,455	11.9%
Wang Lee (5)	10	993	15.4%
TOTAL	9,184	234,292	22.5%

*Krung Thai Bank was formed in 1966, by a merger of the Agricultural Bank (1962 assets of B 1108.1 million) and the Provincial Bank (B 939.5 million).
†Thai Development Bank, 1960–1977
‡Started operations in October 1965
SOURCE: The SGV Group, *A Study of Commercial Banks in Thailand, 1978,* and Alek A. Rozental, op. cit., p. 128.

Central Plains region, it should be noted that deposits originating in Bangkok, in the Plains region, have declined from 72.5 percent of the total in 1966 to 63.5 percent of total deposits at the end of 1978. Since 1976, the Bank of Thailand has sought to expand commercial banks' activities in the provinces by requiring that newly chartered branches provide at least 60 percent of their deposits to finance local activities; of this amount, one-third must be in the form of loans to agriculture.

As noted in an earlier section, Thailand has experienced some increase in banking concentration over time. In particular, the Bangkok Bank, the largest bank in the ASEAN region, has been most successful: its percentage of total commercial bank assets has risen from 25.8 percent in 1962 to 37.9 percent of the domestic bank total at the end of 1978. Using another typical concentration ratio, the share of the top four banks has increased from 60.9 percent in 1962 to 68 percent in 1978. The most rapidly growing commercial bank in Thailand is the Thai Farmers Bank, with a compound growth rate of 28.3

percent; it is currently in third place in terms of assets, followed by the Bangkok Bank at 25.4 percent over the 1962–1978 period. The second largest bank, Krung Thai, largely owned by the government, has been out-distanced by 8 privately owned banks in terms of the rate of growth, suggesting that Thai bankers have been quite skillful in working out their accommodations with the public sector. As Rozental has pointed out: "Every Thai commercial bank has at least one field marshal, general, or member of the royal family on its board, and the political muscle of the Thai banks is an important aspect of the financial nexus."[3]

Among public sector institutions, the central bank, Bank of Thailand (opened in 1942) has total assets of 82.6 billion baht (roughly US$4 billion); it is somewhat smaller than the Bangkok Bank. This fact itself is a tribute to the rather conservative monetary policies of Thai central bankers, since in most LDCs the central bank will be relatively much larger. The Government Savings Bank, whose history dates back to the Government Savings Office of the Finance Ministry in 1913 and to the postal savings system, has total assets of about 20 billion baht and quite an extensive branch network, including mobile banks and floating (or boat) branches.[4] Next, the Bank for Agriculture and Agricultural Cooperatives (BAAC), which dates back to the 1947 Bank for Cooperatives, currently has total assets of 12.6 billion baht; over the past ten years, it has grown at an annual compound rate of about 30 percent per year. The BAAC accepts savings and time deposits, but in recent years an important source of funds has been deposits made by commercial banks, made in order to comply with Bank of Thailand guidelines. While there are a few other government intermediaries in operation, such as the Government Housing Bank, the final institution worth mentioning specifically is the Industrial Finance Corporation of Thailand (IFCT). Established in 1959, it is owned largely by the private sector, but has various lines of credit with the government. Its total assets amount to 2.5 billion baht, and it has also received considerable capital inflows from overseas, both multilateral and bilateral aid.

Foreign bank operations in Thailand are shown in Table 18. It can be seen that considerable shifting has taken place over the past twenty years in the relative importance of the various foreign-chartered banks. In 1962, Chartered Bank was in first place, followed by the Bank of America and Hongkong and Shanghai (the oldest in the

TABLE 18
Foreign Banks in Thailand, 1962–1978

Bank	1962	1966	Growth Rate 1962–66	1978	Growth Rate 1962–78
Chase	179	292	13.0%	2,535	18.5%
Mitsui	212	428	15.1%	2,365	16.3%
Tokyo	37	418	83.0%	2,234	29.3%
Malayan	n.a.	410	n.a.	1,475	11.3%*
Bank of America	325	523	12.7%	1,317	9.1%
Chartered	434	401	neg.	1,273	7.1%
Indochine	131	148	11.1%	1,021	13.7%
Hongkong & Shanghai	295	280	neg.	937	7.6%
China	143	218	3.1%	359	5.9%
Bharat	n.a.	n.a.	n.a.	350	n.a.
Mercantile	138	113	neg.	342	5.8%
European†	n.a.	n.a.	n.a.	294	n.a.
Canton	60	89	10.3%	198	7.8%
Four Seas	n.a.	n.a.	n.a.	194	n.a.
TOTAL	1,954	3,320	14.1%	14,894	13.5%

*Growth rate for 1966–1978 period
†Began operations in July 1978
SOURCE: The SGV Group, *A Study of Commercial Banks in Thailand, 1978,* and Alek A. Rozental, op. cit., pp. 128–132.

kingdom, dating back to 1888). Four years later, the Bank of America was the largest, followed by two Japanese banks and the Malayan Banking Berhad. Now, Chase Manhattan leads the pack, although the highest growth rate of all is exhibited by the Bank of Tokyo, at nearly 30 percent per annum over the entire 1962–1978 period; Chase is second in terms of growth rates, with 18.5 percent per year. It can be seen, however, that foreign bank assets have grown much more slowly than those of their domestic counterparts—the largest foreign bank would rank fourteenth, if included in the listing of all commercial banks. Overall, in 1962 foreign banks accounted for 17.5 percent of total commercial bank assets, but by 1978 this percentage share had shrunk to 6 percent. Curiously, despite this implicit policy of discouraging foreign bank expansion in Thailand, a new commercial bank (European Asian) was chartered in July 1978, while no new local banks have been formed since the mid-1960s.

As noted earlier, finance companies have been among the fastest growing institutions in Thailand's financial system in recent years. Dating back to only around 1969, they have successfully challenged the oligopoly power of the commercial banks in terms of both uses and sources of funds. They currently account for 14.3 percent of total financial assets in Thailand (compared to 67.7 percent for commercial banks), and their promissory notes are competing quite well with commercial bank time deposits, despite the rather stiff requirements covering the minimum amount to be invested. They are subject to Bank of Thailand regulations concerning their "liquidity ratio" and "risk ratio," among others, just like the commercial banks. At the present time, more than 100 finance companies are in operation, many being located in the provinces, where they seem to be able to supply trade credit and medium-term loans with considerably less "red tape" and burdensome collateral requirements than the banks.

In addition to the commercial banking system, a handful of government-sponsored intermediaries, and the finance companies, a sophisticated informal money market exists in Thailand. In rural areas, rice millers often perform elementary banking functions; pawnshops (some government-sponsored) and money-lenders are quite active. As elsewhere in Asia, credit cooperatives of an informal (and technically illegal) sort are found in both rural and urban areas. The "pia-share" or "pia huey" involves a small group of people, often ten to twenty women, who meet regularly to assemble a pool of money for lending to the members. Usually a sealed bid is made for the entire pot, with the highest bidder "paying" an amount equal to the bid into the cooperative treasury. If there are ten people, the first five turn out to be net borrowers and the last five, net lenders. The "share-mother" often taxes a share of the interest total, or borrows the first pool interest-free. Obviously, the people involved must know and trust each other quite completely; but interest earnings of 48 percent or more per year are apparently quite common, which compares quite favorably with 8 to 10 percent offered on long-term time deposits by the organized or official money market.[5]

In recent years, with greater urbanization and mobility, along with somewhat higher interest rates being offered by the commercial banking system, the unorganized money market has probably declined somewhat in relative terms. As Ingram has put it:

> Perhaps the most dramatic monetary change since 1950 is the remarkable growth in time deposits. Beginning at a near-zero level in 1950, time deposits rose slowly during the 1950's, reaching only 1.66 billion baht in 1959, but they then grew rapidly to 20.07 billion baht in 1969. By 1969 time deposits were approximately equal to the total money supply. . . . This phenomenal increase in privately held time deposits

reflects the increasing monetization of the economy, but more than that it indicates a growth in private saving and public confidence in both the baht and the banking system.[6]

Total time and savings deposits have continued their phenomenal expansion: from 20 billion baht in 1969, the total has risen to 132.7 billion baht at the end of 1978, a compound annual growth rate of approximately 24 percent. The money supply at the end of 1978 only stood at 52.9 billion baht, giving Thailand the highest ratio of M2 to M1 in the ASEAN region. In addition to the improved public confidence thesis put forth by Ingram, one might also note that non-bank financial intermediaries (cooperatives, insurance companies, savings banks, and the like) and securities markets[7] are rather less well-developed than the commercial banks in Thailand. Also, this time deposit growth is associated with Thailand's underdeveloped pension system, suburbanization, and rapid expansion in automobile ownership. (Home mortgages and hire-purchase plans have become available only recently, and many people still hope to save up the full amount.)

Table 19 summarizes the sectoral flow of funds from the commercial banking system and from Thailand's finance companies in 1978; as noted above, these two financial sectors account for more than 80 percent of total financial assets in the kingdom. Commercial banks, in particular, tend to be performing much as in the past, lending to

TABLE 19
Sectoral Credit Allocation in Thailand, 1978
(percent of lending)

Sector	Commercial Banks	Finance Companies
Agriculture	4.3	1.1
Mining	1.2	0.6
Manufacturing	18.2	26.7
Construction	4.5	4.4
Real estate	3.8	5.0
Imports	13.9	5.3
Exports	13.0	1.7
Wholesale/Retail	21.6	14.0
Utilities	1.3	1.0
Finance	6.1	15.2
Services	4.2	4.6
Personal Consumption	7.9	20.4

SOURCE: Surasak Nananukool, "Role of Financial Institutions in Economic Development," p. 422.

established customers in the traditional fields of export–import and wholesale–retail trade. Despite the fact that the Bank of Thailand target for agricultural lending is now in the 11 to 13 percent range, the end results in 1978 fell short badly, with only 4.3 percent of bank credit going to agriculture. As Surasak Nananukool, Manager of Bangkok Bank's Office of Domestic Credit, tries to explain:

> A major obstacle in this field is that interest rates on agricultural loans are low, being only 12–13 per cent. If the rate were raised to 15 per cent, it might still not cover risk and expenses. Extending agricultural credits requires a bigger staff than business credit. In addition, the agricultural sector still depends largely on the weather for the success of its crops, so this attitude to the low rate of interest is not felt only at head-office level; even branch managers who must maximize profits and minimize bad debts using a small staff naturally try to avoid giving this type of credit.[8]

This, of course, leads to the perverse flow of credit from the provinces to Bangkok, and forces the agricultural sector either to turn to the informal money market, with its rates of 48 to 72 percent, or to forego using modern inputs for which cash is needed. While it would be presumptuous for an outsider to offer unsolicited advice from a great distance, the greater use of cooperatives, crop insurance schemes, and some relaxation in the banker's penchant for detailed documentation are all components of an answer. Further study of more successful agricultural credit systems (those of Japan, Taiwan, Korea, perhaps of Australia and New Zealand) should prove fruitful on this score. It was rather shocking to hear that the Bank of Thailand had proposed to set up a special fund to bail out an ailing stock exchange in 1979 when sectoral and regional credit allocation seems to need special assistance most. And to do that in the government-proclaimed Year of the Farmer!

NOTES

1. Since 1972, the minimum "deposit" with a finance company is 50,000 baht ($2,500) in Bangkok and 10,000 baht outside Bangkok. It may be noted that even the latter figure is somewhat above Thailand's annual per capita income.

2. Alek A. Rozental, *Finance and Development in Thailand*.

3. Ibid., p. 349.

4. For further detail, cf. Robert F. Emery, *The Financial Institutions of Southeast Asia*, pp. 613–619.

5. For some further discussion of these "rotating-credit" societies, see Robert F.

Emery, *Financial Institutions,* pp. 603–605, as well as Alek A. Rozental, *Finance and Development,* pp. 269–272.

6. James C. Ingram, *Economic Change in Thailand Since 1850,* p. 307.

7. At the present time, about fifty firms are listed on the Securities Exchange of Thailand. Until 1977, turnover was miniscule, but it jumped to 26.6 billion baht that year. See *Securities Exchange of Thailand, 1978-1979 Handbook,* p. 39. The insurance industry has also had great difficulties in getting started, due to company failures in the 1960s.

8. *Bangkok Bank Monthly Review, loc. cit.* For a more general discussion, cf. Dale W. Adams, "Mobilizing Household Saving through Rural Financial Markets," pp. 547–560 and Dale W. Adams and G. I. Nehman, "Borrowing Costs and the Demand for Rural Credit," pp. 165–176.

CHAPTER 8
Summary

The problem of underdevelopment—the root cause of "third world" poverty—has been approached from a number of very different points of view during the thirty-year history of the development economics subfield. One school of thought, including but not limited to the Marxists, views poverty in the LDCs as being caused largely by external factors. This approach argues that the international trade and finance system is permanently biased against the poor countries of the world, and that the rich countries have improved their living standards at their expense. The problem of raw material versus industrial product prices seems to be a cornerstone in this argument, but the importance of colonial exploitation and imperialism is also always noted. Since the South is poor because the North is rich, according to this view, the LDCs should withdraw from international trade, refuse exploitative foreign investment, and insist on large inter-governmental resource transfers to rectify past injustices. In terms of domestic policy, the development of import-substitution industries is stressed, and the public sector usually overrules world market prices and takes over most of the allocation process. However, economically, most countries adopting this view have done rather poorly; a particularly galling development for these "world economy" theorists must be the recent decisions in mainland China that imply that the benefits of foreign trade and investment probably outweigh the costs. The repudiation of Sukarno in Indonesia, the recent change of climate in Sri Lanka, and feelers being extended to the industrial countries by both Burma and Vietnam are additional bits of evidence on this score.

The alternative to this world economy view of underdevelopment might be termed the "traditional society" approach. To borrow a term from the Chinese equivalent of an elementary economics text, most "vulgar bourgeois economists" would probably agree that the constraints on economic growth are largely internal. Political, social, and cultural factors are very important, while an inadequate savings-investment level, population pressure, and a lack of entrepreneurship are economic barriers to modernization. In Asia, particularly, the success stories of Japan, Taiwan, Korea, and a number of the ASEAN countries have all been built upon export-oriented economies, so that the foreign trade system apparently cannot be a wholly negative influence. Furthermore, integration of a rapidly growing economy into the international trade network does not seem to require surrendering national sovereignty (Japan certainly has not) nor does it necessarily involve a more unequal distribution of income as an inevitable consequence of rapid growth (as Korea proves). In some ASEAN countries, remarkable rates of export growth have been coupled with further immiserization of the rural poor (Indonesia), but in others this has not been the case (in Malaysia and Thailand, though available evidence is sketchy).

What has been established as a result of the past three decades of development experience is that (1) economic growth is closely related to national savings-investment levels, (2) domestic saving is quantitatively more important than the inflow of foreign capital, and (3) financial institutions can play an important role in savings mobilization and credit allocation. A fourth tentative finding is that competition among financial institutions and positive real interest rates assist in the monetization process and lead to a further diversification in financial asset holdings.

It has been found that saving rises somewhat more than proportionately as per capita income expands. One plausible explanation is simply monetization: "as money replaces barter for transactions, the public wish[es] to hold a higher proportion of their income in the form of money which they can only do by giving up command over real resources." Another possibility is that population growth levels off as per capita income rises, or that the distribution of income becomes somewhat more unequal as income goes up, but at a decreasing rate. In any case, Thirlwall finds that the savings ratio reaches a maximum of about 25 percent at a per capita income of $2,000.[1] During the past twenty years, the saving performance of the developing countries taken as a group has been quite impressive: the saving rate as a proportion of GDP has risen from about 12.8 percent in 1951-1960 to about 17.0 percent in 1961-1970. On the other hand, "the foreign saving rate was around 2.2% of GDP for all the LDCs during 1961-70, financing only about 11-12% of gross investment."[2] Foreign borrowing does not appear very attractive politically for many LDCs, and a number of Asian countries seem to be approaching limits of prudence in this regard. To quote Bhatt and Meerman:

> Short-term borrowing on the 1974-75 scale, even if feasible, cannot continue without giving hostages to fortune—this can only be an immediate temporary response to a factor that requires more viable and sustainable adaptation. So investment levels and hence growth of incomes cannot be maintained without a compensating rise in the domestic saving rate—hence, the urgency of policy measures to improve the level and allocation of domestic resources.[3]

This same point was made even more forcefully by Ragnar Nurkse twenty-five years ago:

> A nation cannot be strongly capital-conscious unless the individuals that compose it do some saving of their own and can see from their own experience the point of roundabout methods of production. If this requisite is not fulfilled foreign business capital is apt to remain a mere projection of the creditor economy. Direct foreign investment in these circumstances is not always a happy form of cultural contact, and this aspect of it may lie at the root of some of the trouble in which it has often resulted.[4]

During the past thirty years of development experience, excessive emphasis has also been placed on the role of the public sector. Most bilateral aid programs have insisted on a rising ratio of taxes to national income (often called the "self-help" ratio), and endless man-hours have been spent to prove that one dollar of A.I.D. money mobilizes local government spending of additional funds (the "aid multiplier"). Indeed, rising tax ratios have been cited as a success story by representatives of multilateral agencies as well,[5] and it is often said that one of the standard recommendations of an IMF or an

IBRD mission is that taxes should be raised. Yet, the bulk of government revenue goes to support government consumption rather than development investment. The efficiency record of most public sector enterprises is not a happy one, and the overall level of public-sector saving is rather small—2 to 3 percent of GNP.[6]

The experience of Japan is cited by Bhatt and Meerman as being potentially relevant to most LDCs: in Japan, the non-corporate sector saves about 21 percent of disposable income (compared to only about 7 percent in the U.S.). Fully 80 percent of financial saving is in the form of deposits in banks and other institutions. Bhatt and Meerman cite four factors as being explanatory.[7]

1. There exists a bank office for approximately every 10,000 Japanese. There are also about 7,000 offices of credit associations and credit cooperatives, and almost an equal number of cooperatives in the agricultural sector. Finally, the postal savings system has more than 20,000 offices.

2. Positive real interest rates are offered (a real rate of about 3 percent for a one-year bank deposit).

3. Banks aggressively promote saving by programs such as gifts to depositors, door-to-door solicitation, and lottery deposits (which could have a special appeal in a number of ASEAN countries).

4. Government policies to ensure safety—supervision and deposit insurance.

In conclusion, we have seen that monetization and financial deepening have been taking place quite rapidly in all of the ASEAN countries, especially in Singapore, the hub of the regional financial system. Sixto Roxas has computed Goldsmith's financial assets/GNP ratios for the ASEAN, which are reproduced below.[8]

	Indonesia	Malaysia	Philippines	Singapore	Thailand
1967	23	71	76	94	52
1974	56	113	122	378	75

Despite inflation and political uncertainties, mobilization of savings seems to be accelerating quite rapidly; holdings of M2 per capita have grown enormously in terms of local currency as well as in real or foreign exchange terms. Commercial banks dominate the financial sectors of the ASEAN countries. Public sector intermediaries have been used productively in some cases (Malaysia's EPF), but have been a deterrent to efficiency in some others (Indonesia's state banks). Generally, credit allocation has not paid sufficient attention to the agricultural sector; however, specialized intermediaries have been set up and are expanding rapidly in some cases (e.g., Thailand's BAAC). Non-banking intermediaries (savings and loans, mutual funds, insurance and pension plans) still await development, and a long-term capital market cannot be said to exist. Nevertheless, the relatively open ASEAN economies and their financial institutions can probably serve as a model for the more backward Third World countries currently searching for viable development strategies.

Looking to the future of the ASEAN countries, an optimist can foresee favorable developments in economic cooperation and even monetary integration. It is possible to point to the emergence of special trading preferences, initiatives in cooperative project design (the famous five projects of 1976), and relative stability of exchange rates among the ASEAN countries. Privately owned financial institutions continue to exist as viable entities; businessmen and bureaucrats travel easily between ASEAN capitals, and there seems to be an ASEAN consensus position on most "Third World" issues. Central bank cooperation seems to promise an eventual coordination of economic policies, and it is possible to talk about an eventual monetary union. More pessimistically, it should be noted that the European Economic Community is still well short of having a common currency after more than two decades of cooperative efforts; and also that national interests tend to overshadow regional concerns in contemporary ASEAN negotiations. Still, the Europeans have come up with the European Monetary System and the European Currency Unit in recent years. The free market economies of Asia might not be very far behind.

NOTES

1. See A. P. Thirlwall, *Inflation, Saving and Growth in Developing Economies*, pp. 164–165. Thirlwall fitted a parabola to data for sixty-three countries and got the following results:

$$\frac{S}{Y} = 10.675 + \underset{(0.0017)}{0.0149} \left[\frac{Y}{N}\right] - \underset{(0.0000006)}{0.0000038} \left[\frac{Y}{N}\right]^2.$$

The R^2 was 0.622 and the standard errors are given in parentheses. For evidence specifically from Asia, see Jeffrey G. Williamson, "Personal Saving in Developing Nations," pp. 194–210.

2. V. V. Bhatt and Jacob Meerman, "Resource Mobilization in Developing Countries: Financial Institutions and Policies," pp. 45–46.

3. Ibid., p. 46.

4. Ragnar Nurkse, *Problems of Capital Formation in Underdeveloped Countries,* p. 156.

5. V. V. Bhatt and Jacob Meerman, "Resource Mobilization," pp. 48–49.

6. Ibid., p. 52.

7. Ibid., p. 53.

8. Sixto K. Roxas, *Managing Asian Financial Development,* p. 207. For reference, the ratio for the U.S. is 152 and for Japan it is 180 (for 1973).

Bibliography

Abdi, Ali Issa, *Commercial Banks and Economic Development: The Experience of Eastern Africa* (New York: Praeger, 1978).

Adams, Dale W., "Mobilizing Household Saving through Rural Financial Markets," *Economic Development and Cultural Change,* April 1978, pp. 547–560.

_____, and G. I. Nehman, "Borrowing Costs and the Demand for Rural Credit," *Journal of Development Studies,* January 1979, pp. 165–176.

Adams, T. F. M., and Iwao Hashii, *A Financial History of the New Japan* (Tokyo: Kodansha International, Ltd., 1972).

Aghevli, Bijan B., "A Model of the Monetary Sector for Indonesia, 1968–1973," *Bulletin of Indonesian Economic Studies,* November 1976, pp. 50–60.

_____, "Money, Prices, and the Balance of Payments: Indonesia, 1968–73," *Journal of Development Studies,* January 1977, pp. 37–58.

Arndt, H. W., "Survey of Recent Developments," *Bulletin of Indonesian Economic Studies,* March 1978, pp. 1–28.

Baldwin, Robert E., *The Philippines: Foreign Trade Regimes and Economic Development,* Vol. V (New York: Columbia University Press for the National Bureau of Economic Research, 1975).

Bank Negara Malaysia (Economic Research and Statistics Department), *Money and Banking in Malaysia, 1959–1979* (Kuala Lumpur: Bank Negara Malaysia, 1979).

Basch, Antonin, *Financing Economic Development* (New York: Macmillan, 1964).

Bennett, Robert L., *The Financial Sector and Economic Development: The Mexican Case* (Baltimore, Md.: The Johns Hopkins University Press, 1965).

Bhatia, Rattan J., and Deena R. Khatkhate, "Financial Intermediation, Savings Mobilization, and Entrepreneurial Development: The African Experience," *IMF Staff Papers,* March 1975, pp. 132–158.

Bhatt, V. V., and Jacob Meerman. "Resource Mobilization in Developing Countries: Financial Institutions and Policies," *World Development,* January 1978, pp. 45–64.

Bilsborrow, Richard E., "Age Distribution and Savings Rates in Less Developed Countries," *Economic Development and Cultural Change,* October 1979, pp. 23–45.

Blumenthal, Tuvia, *Savings in Postwar Japan* (Cambridge, Mass.: Harvard University Press, 1970).

Caldwell, J. Alexander, "The Financial System in Taiwan: Structure, Functions, and Issues for the Future," *Asian Survey,* August 1976, pp. 729–751.

Cameron, Rondo, ed., *Banking and Economic Development* (New York: Oxford University Press, 1972).

————, *Banking in the Early Stages of Industrialization* (New York: Oxford University Press, 1967).

Chandavarkar, Anand G., "Some Aspects of Interest Rate Policies in Less Developed Economies: The Experience of Selected Asian Countries," *IMF Staff Papers,* March 1971, pp. 48–112.

————, "Monetization of Developing Economies," *IMF Staff Papers,* November 1978, pp. 665–721.

Collis, Maurice, *Wayfoong: the Hongkong and Shanghai Banking Corporation* (London: Faber and Faber, Ltd., 1965).

Cruz, Roman A., Jr., "Monetary Policy and Economic Development," *The Philippine Economy in the 1970's,* University of the Philippines, Institute of Economic Development and Research, in cooperation with the Private Development Corporation of the Philippines, 1972.

Dick, Howard, "Survey of Recent Developments," *Bulletin of Indonesian Economic Studies,* March 1979, pp. 1–44.

Drake, P. J., *Financial Development in Malaya and Singapore* (Canberra: Australian National University Press, 1969).

————, "Securities Markets in Less-Developed Countries," *Journal of Development Studies,* January 1977, pp. 73–91.

Emery, R. F., *The Financial Institutions of Southeast Asia* (New York: Praeger, 1970).

Far Eastern Economic Review, *Asia Yearbook, 1979.*

Fisk, E. K., "The Justification and Assessment of Small Loans by Development Banking Institutions," *Malayan Economic Review,* April 1975, pp. 1–11.

Freeman, Roger A., *Socialism and Private Enterprise in Equatorial Asia: The Case of Malaysia and Indonesia* (Stanford: The Hoover Institute on War, Revolution, and Peace, 1968).

Galbis, Vicente, "Financial Intermediation and Economic Growth in Less-Developed Countries: A Theoretical Approach," *Journal of Development Studies,* January 1977, pp. 58–72.

Garnaut, Ross, ed., *ASEAN in a Changing Pacific and World Economy* (Canberra: Australian National University Press, forthcoming).

Goldsmith, Raymond W., *Financial Structure and Development* (New Haven: Yale University Press, 1969).

Grenville, Stephen, "Commercial Banks and Money Creation," *Bulletin of Indonesian Economic Studies,* March 1977, pp. 75–94.

Gurley, John G., and Edward S. Shaw, "Financial Development and Economic Development," *Economic Development and Cultural Change,* April 1967, pp. 257–268.

———, *Money in a Theory of Finance* (Washington, D.C.: The Brookings Institution, 1960).

Hainsworth, Geoffrey B., "Economic Growth and Poverty in Southeast Asia: Malaysia, Indonesia, and the Philippines," *Pacific Affairs,* Spring 1979, pp. 5–41.

Hodjera, Zoran, "The Asian Currency Market: Singapore as a Regional Financial Center," *IMF Staff Papers,* June 1978, pp. 221–247.

Ingram, James C., *Economic Change in Thailand Since 1850* (Stanford, Ca.: Stanford University Press, 1971).

International Bank for Reconstruction and Development, *The Philippines: Priorities and Prospects for Development* (Washington, D.C.: The World Bank, 1976).

Jao, Y. C., "Financial Deepening and Economic Growth: A Cross-Section Analysis," *The Malayan Economic Review,* June 1976, pp. 47–57.

Kasper, Wolfgang, *Malaysia: A Study in Successful Economic Development* (Washington, D.C.: American Enterprise Institute, 1974).

Kelley, Allen C., and Jeffrey G. Williamson, "Household Behavior in the Developing Economies: The Indonesian Case," *Economic Development and Cultural Change,* April 1968, pp. 385–403.

Laumas, Prem S., "Monetization, Economic Development and the Demand for Money," *Review of Economics and Statistics,* November 1978, pp. 614–618.

Lee Hock Lock, *Household Saving in West Malaysia and the Problem of Financing Economic Development* (Kuala Lumpur: University of Malaya, February 1971).

Leff, Nathaniel H., "Industrial Organization and Entrepreneurship in the Developing Countries: The Economic Groups," *Economic Development and Cultural Change,* July 1978, pp. 661–675.

Lim, David, *Economic Growth and Development in West Malaysia, 1947–1970* (Kuala Lumpur: Oxford University Press, 1973).

Lipton, Michael, "Agricultural Finance and Rural Credit in Poor Countries," *World Development,* July 1976, pp. 543–554.

———, *Why Poor People Stay Poor: Urban Bias in World Development* (London: Temple Smith, 1977).

McKinnon, Ronald I., *Money and Capital in Economic Development* (Washington, D.C.: Brookings Institution, 1973).

———, ed., *Money and Finance in Economic Growth and Development* (New York: Marcel Dekker, Inc., 1976).

Mortimer, Rex, ed., *Showcase State: The Illusion of Indonesia's "Accelerated Modernization"* (Sydney: Angus and Robertson, 1973).

Muscat, Robert J., *Development Strategy in Thailand* (New York: Praeger, 1966).

Nananukool, Surak, "Role of Financial Institutions in Economic Development," *Bangkok Bank Monthly Review,* October–November 1979, pp. 421–424.

Newlyn, W. T. et al., *The Financing of Economic Development* (Oxford: Clarendon Press, 1977).

Nisbet, Charles, "Interest Rates and Imperfect Competition in the Informal Credit Market of Rural Chile," *Economic Development and Cultural Change*, October 1967, pp. 73–90.

Nurkse, Ragnar, *Problems of Capital Formation in Underdeveloped Countries* (Oxford: Basil Blackwell, 1955).

Owens, Edgar, and Robert Shaw, *Development Reconsidered* (Lexington, Mass.: D. C. Heath and Co., 1974).

Patrick, Hugh T., "Financial Development and Economic Growth in Underdeveloped Countries," *Economic Development and Cultural Change*, January 1966, pp. 174–189.

Park, Yung Chul, "The Role of Money in Stabilization Policy in Developing Countries," *IMF Staff Papers*, July 1973, pp. 379–418.

Porter, Richard C., "The Promotion of the 'Banking Habit' and Economic Development," *Journal of Development Studies*, July 1966, pp. 346–366.

Roxas, Sixto K., *Managing Asian Financial Development* (Metro Manila: Sinag-Tala Publishers, Inc., 1976).

Rozental, Alek A., *Finance and Development in Thailand* (New York: Praeger, 1970).

Sametz, Arnold W., ed., *Financial Development and Economic Growth* (New York: New York University Press, 1972).

Securities Exchange of Thailand, 1978-1979 Handbook (Bangkok: S.E.T., 1979).

Shaw, Edward S., *Financial Deepening in Economic Development* (New York: Oxford University Press, 1973).

Tanzi, Vito, "Fiscal Policy, Keynesian Economics, and the Mobilization of Savings in Developing Countries," *World Development*, October–November 1976, pp. 907–917.

Thirlwall, A. P., *Inflation, Saving, and Growth in Developing Economies* (London: Macmillan, 1974).

———, *Financing Economic Development* (London: Macmillan, 1976).

Tun Wai, U, *Financial Intermediation and National Savings in Developing Countries* (New York: Praeger, 1972).

———, "Interest Rates in the Organized Money Markets of Underdeveloped Countries," *IMF Staff Papers*, August 1956, pp. 249–278.

———, "Stock and Bond Issues and Capital Markets in Less Developed Countries," *IMF Staff Papers*, July 1973, pp. 253–317.

Vasey, Lloyd R., ed., *ASEAN and a Positive Strategy for Foreign Investment* (Honolulu: The University Press of Hawaii for the Pacific Forum, 1978).

———, and G. J. Viksnins, eds., *The Economic and Political Growth Pattern of Asia Pacific* (Honolulu: The University Press of Hawaii for the Pacific Forum, 1976).

Williamson, Jeffrey G., "Why Do Koreans Save 'So Little?' " *Journal of Development Economics*, September 1979, pp. 343–362.

———, "Personal Saving in Developing Nations: An Intertemporal Cross-section from Asia," *Economic Record*, June 1968, pp. 194–210.

Yotopoulos, P. A., and J. B. Nugent, *The Economics of Development: Empirical Investigations* (New York: McGraw-Hill, 1978).

DATE